ROMANS

Even the most unlikely people can experience radical unity.

THIS BOOK BELONGS TO

_____

START DATE

_____

SHE READS TRUTH

FOUNDERS

FOUNDER
Raechel Myers

CO-FOUNDER
Amanda Bible Williams

EXECUTIVE

CHIEF EXECUTIVE OFFICER
Ryan Myers

CHIEF BRAND & MARKETING OFFICER
Amy Dennis

CHIEF CONTENT OFFICER
Jessica Lamb

CHIEF OPERATING OFFICER
Raechel Myers

EDITORIAL

DIGITAL MANAGING EDITOR
Oghosa Iyamu, MDiv

PRODUCTION EDITOR
Hannah Little, MTS

MARKETING CONTENT EDITOR
Tameshia Williams, ThM

ASSOCIATE EDITORS
Kayla De La Torre, MAT
Lindsey Jacobi, MDiv

COPY EDITOR
Becca Owens, MA

MARKETING

MARKETING DIRECTOR
Kamron Kunce

GROWTH MARKETING MANAGER
Blake Showalter

PRODUCT MARKETING MANAGER
Megan Phillips

SOCIAL MEDIA STRATEGIST
Taylor Krupp

CREATIVE

DESIGN MANAGER
Kelsea Allen

DESIGNERS
Abbey Benson
Amanda Brush, MA
Annie Glover
Lauren Haag

JUNIOR DESIGNER
Jessie Gerakinis

OPERATIONS

OPERATIONS DIRECTOR
Allison Sutton

OFFICE MANAGER
Nicole Quirion

PROJECT ASSISTANT
Mary Beth Montgomery

SHIPPING

SHIPPING MANAGER
Marian Byne

FULFILLMENT LEAD
Cait Baggerman

FULFILLMENT SPECIALIST
Hannah Lamb
Kajsa Matheny
Lauren Neal

SUBSCRIPTION INQUIRIES
orders@shereadstruth.com

COMMUNITY SUPPORT

COMMUNITY EXPERIENCE DIRECTOR
Kara Hewett, MOL

COMMUNITY SUPPORT SPECIALISTS
Katy McKnight
Alecia Rohrer
Heather Vollono

@SHEREADSTRUTH

 Download the She Reads Truth app, available for iOS and Android

  Subscribe to the She Reads Truth podcast

SHEREADSTRUTH.COM

This book was printed offset in Nashville, Tennessee, on 70# Lynx Opaque. Cover is 100# Cougar Opaque with a soft touch lamination.

Lindsey

Lindsey Jacobi, MDiv
ASSOCIATE EDITOR

Take a minute to put yourself in first-century sandals as a part of the Christian community in Rome. Think about the struggles, persecutions, and the day-in and day-out challenges of growing the Church in a world that opposed the new message of Jesus.

Now picture gathering in a friend's main room with other believers. It's a room full of brothers and sisters in Christ who have different backgrounds, wounds, experiences, and convictions than you, but the same faith. Your group has gotten word from a faithful leader who has been doing gospel work in cities far and wide. Paul, the persecutor-turned-radical disciple, has sent a letter to the believers in Rome. So you gather together to hear what he has to say. And sitting there, in a room of women, men, slaves, Roman citizens, immigrants, and poor and wealthy believers, a faithful benefactor and sister in the faith, Phoebe, shares with you all words of rich, gospel reminders.

Where we might read Romans today as a robust theological treatise, full of ten dollar spiritual words, the Christians in Rome would have experienced this letter from Paul as practical encouragement born out of theological truth. The diverse gatherings of believers in Rome had challenges, just like any church of its day or ours. Jewish and Gentile Christians weren't on the same page about how their faith played out in practice. Did the Gentiles have to conform to the law? How were both groups going to coexist with different understandings of how to live out their faith? (Take a look at "The Christian Church in Rome" on page 146 for more about the original recipients of this letter.)

Paul's words of encouragement about the salvation and grace of Jesus Christ are a reminder that even the most unlikely people can experience radical unity. We discover in Romans that, when we keep the main things the main things, those differences don't have to divide us. The points on which we build our faith are the aspects that unify us. After all, every one of us is a former prisoner who has been set free because of Christ. All who claim Jesus for salvation stand in His righteousness, His sacrifice, and His grace extended to unworthy sinners.

So come to the book of Romans with fresh eyes for the journey ahead. Imagine what it would have been like to sit and hear Phoebe share these words of grace, truth, and challenge from Paul. Remember in this reading of Romans the good news for you that is the gospel of Jesus—the freedom and new life that we get to live out because of it. I pray it sinks into our bones, informing and infusing every corner of our lives as we walk in faith.

Design on Purpose

At She Reads Truth, we believe in pairing the inherently beautiful Word of God with the aesthetic beauty it deserves. Each of our resources is thoughtfully and artfully designed to highlight the beauty, goodness, and truth of Scripture in a way that reflects the themes of each curated reading plan.

For the design of this Study Book, we used a variety of substances from the earth, like sand, salt, dirt, clay, and more to create unique pieces of artwork. The variety of elements were chosen to represent the array of people who made up the Christian church in Rome. These varied materials and textures work together to create each design, reflecting how different followers of Christ come together to form a unified body. Even as their experiences, backgrounds, and convictions remain distinct, the combined group is a rich picture of true freedom in Christ. These natural elements root us in the time and space in which the letter to the Romans was originally given and the lived nature of the gospel.

HOW TO USE THIS BOOK

She Reads Truth is a community of women dedicated to reading
the Word of God every day. In this **Romans** reading plan,
we will read Romans, along with complementary passages
of Scripture, as we explore the gospel message of hope and
salvation through Jesus Christ.

READ & REFLECT

Your **Romans** Study Book
focuses primarily on Scripture,
with added features to come
alongside your time with
God's Word.

SCRIPTURE READING

Designed for a Monday start, this
Study Book presents the book of
Romans in daily readings, along with
additional passages curated to show
how the theme of the main reading
can be found throughout Scripture.

◢ *Additional passages are marked
in your daily reading with the Going
Deeper heading.*

REFLECTION QUESTIONS

Each week features response questions
and space for personal reflection.

COMMUNITY & CONVERSATION

You can start reading this book at any time!
If you want to join women from Salem to Spain
as they read along with you, the She Reads Truth
community will start Day 1 of **Romans** on
Monday, July 10, 2023.

 SHE READS TRUTH APP

Devotionals corresponding to each daily reading can be
found in the **Romans** reading plan on the She Reads Truth
app. Devotionals will be published each weekday once the
plan begins on Monday, July 10, 2023. You can use the
app to participate in community discussion and more.

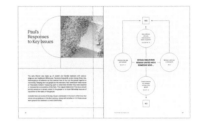

GRACE DAY

Use Saturdays to catch up on your reading, pray, and rest in the presence of the Lord.

WEEKLY TRUTH

Sundays are set aside for Scripture memorization.

See tips for memorizing Scripture on page 164.

EXTRAS

This book features additional tools to help you gain a deeper understanding of the text.

Find a complete list of extras on page 13.

 SHEREADSTRUTH.COM

The **Romans** reading plan and devotionals will also be available at SheReadsTruth.com as the community reads each day. Invite your family, friends, and neighbors to read along with you!

 SHE READS TRUTH PODCAST

Subscribe to the She Reads Truth podcast and join our founders and their guests each week as they talk about what you'll read in the week ahead.

*Podcast episodes 185–189 for our **Romans** series release on Mondays beginning July 10, 2023.*

Table of Contents

WEEK 1

WEEK 2

WEEK 3

WEEK 4

EXTRAS

WEEK 5

For all have sinned and fall short of the glory of God; they are justified freely by his grace through the redemption that is in Christ Jesus.

ROMANS

SHE READS

Romans

TIME TO READ ROMANS: 57 Minutes

ON THE TIMELINE

The indisputable author of the book of Romans is the apostle Paul. Paul was a former persecutor of the early Church who, after becoming a follower of Jesus, brought this good news to non-Jewish people (Gentiles) and wrote several of the New Testament letters. From the book of Acts and statements made in Romans, we learn that Paul wrote the letter to the Romans while he was in Corinth in the spring of AD 57, where he stopped on his way to Jerusalem to deliver an offering from the Gentile churches to poor Jewish Christians (Ac 20:3; Rm 15:25–29). This places the writing of Romans at the end of Paul's third missionary journey. (Turn to page 50 to see the route Paul took on this missionary journey.)

A LITTLE BACKGROUND

The imposing city of Rome was the primary destination for this letter. Some manuscripts, however, lack the phrase "in Rome" (Rm 1:7), giving some support to the conclusion that Paul intended an even wider audience for the letter. The origin of the Roman house churches is unknown, though their foundations can be traced back to the "visitors from Rome (both Jews and converts)" who came to Jerusalem at Pentecost (Ac 2:10), many of whom converted to Christianity (Ac 2:41).

MESSAGE & PURPOSE

Paul's letter to the Roman house churches has been a favorite among the New Testament writings for its theological and pastoral influence. It focuses on the doctrine of salvation, including the practical implications for believers as they live out the salvation given to them through Jesus Christ. Paul's purpose in writing the letter was to impart spiritual strength to the believers in Rome (Rm 1:11–12; 16:25–26). Paul also hoped to enlist the Roman churches to support a mission to the west (Rm 15:23–29). He asked for prayer for the difficult task he was undertaking (Rm 15:30–31) and that he might be able to visit them (Rm 15:32). In response to Jewish-Gentile tensions (read more about this on page 116), Paul included an exposition of what is essential to Christianity and what is not.

GIVE THANKS FOR THE BOOK OF ROMANS

In the book of Romans, Paul emphasized righteousness and justification by grace through faith to a depth and detail not found elsewhere in the Bible. Paul also mapped out the spread of human sin and its results for both believers and nonbelievers. In Romans 6–8, Paul gave a comprehensive development of our union with Christ and the Spirit's work in us.

Why Did Paul Write Romans?

Desire

Paul had long wanted to go to Rome so that he could encourage and strengthen the Roman believers by reminding them of the truth, nature, and implications of the gospel.

Rm 1:9—15

Care

Paul heard tensions existed between the believers in Rome (see page 116 for more on these differences). Paul wanted to address these issues that divided them and show them a way to live unified in Christ. He was reminding them of the foundation of the gospel message and how it should shape their lives.

Rm 9:30—10:4; 16:17—18

Vision

Paul wanted to eventually take the gospel to Spain and hoped Rome would become his base of operations, as Antioch had been for his first three missionary journeys.

Rm 15:22—24

Plan

Paul intended to visit Rome as soon as he delivered an offering to the poor believers in Jerusalem.

Rm 15:25—29

Opportunity

Paul knew his friend Phoebe could deliver his letter. Phoebe was from the city of Cenchreae, which was near Corinth. She was likely near Paul when he was writing his letter to the Romans.

Rm 16:1—4

Not Ashamed of the Gospel

For I am not ashamed
of the gospel, because
it is the power of
God for salvation to
everyone who believes.

ROMANS 1:16

ROMANS 1:1–17

The Gospel of God for Rome

¹ Paul, a servant of Christ Jesus, called as an apostle and set apart for the gospel of God— ² which he promised beforehand through his prophets in the Holy Scriptures— ³ concerning his Son, Jesus Christ our Lord, who was a descendant of David according to the flesh ⁴ and was appointed to be the powerful Son of God according to the Spirit of holiness by the resurrection of the dead. ⁵ Through him we have received grace and apostleship to bring about the obedience of faith for the sake of his name among all the Gentiles, ⁶ including you who are also called by Jesus Christ.

⁷ To all who are in Rome, loved by God, called as saints.

Grace to you and peace from God our Father and the Lord Jesus Christ.

Paul's Desire to Visit Rome

⁸ First, I thank my God through Jesus Christ for all of you because the news of your faith is being reported in all the world. ⁹ God is my witness, whom I serve with my spirit in telling the good news about his Son—that I constantly mention you, ¹⁰ always asking in my prayers that if it is somehow in God's will, I may now at last succeed in coming to you. ¹¹ For I want very much to see you, so that I may impart to you some spiritual gift to strengthen you, ¹² that is, to be mutually encouraged by each other's faith, both yours and mine.

¹³ Now I don't want you to be unaware, brothers and sisters, that I often planned to come to you (but was prevented until now) in order that I might have a fruitful ministry among you, just as I have had among the rest of the Gentiles. ¹⁴ I am obligated both to Greeks and barbarians, both to the wise and the foolish. ¹⁵ So I am eager to preach the gospel to you also who are in Rome.

The Righteous Will Live by Faith

¹⁶ For I am not ashamed of the gospel, because it is the power of God for salvation to everyone who believes, first to the Jew, and also to the Greek. ¹⁷ For in it the righteousness of God is revealed from faith to faith, just as it is written: The righteous will live by faith.

❤ GOING DEEPER

PSALM 40:9–10

⁹ I proclaim righteousness in the great assembly;
see, I do not keep my mouth closed—
as you know, LORD.

When you see underlined words or phrases, read the description and turn to the map on page 50 to help you visualize where these events occurred.

Paul wrote to the Roman church while he was in Corinth.

Paul was called by God to go to Rome while he was in Jerusalem (Ac 23:11).

¹⁰ I did not hide your righteousness in my heart;
I spoke about your faithfulness and salvation;
I did not conceal your constant love and truth
from the great assembly.

MARK 8:34–38

Take Up Your Cross

³⁴ Calling the crowd along with his disciples, he said to them, "If anyone wants to follow after me, let him deny himself, take up his cross, and follow me. ³⁵ For whoever wants to save his life will lose it, but whoever loses his life because of me and the gospel will save it. ³⁶ For what does it benefit someone to gain the whole world and yet lose his life? ³⁷ What can anyone give in exchange for his life? ³⁸ For whoever is ashamed of me and my words in this adulterous and sinful generation, the Son of Man will also be ashamed of him when he comes in the glory of his Father with the holy angels."

NOTES ———————— DAY 01

Exchanging the Truth for a Lie

DAY ———————————————————— 02

They exchanged the
truth of God for a lie...

ROMANS 1:25

The Guilt of the Gentile World

[18] For God's wrath is revealed from heaven against all godlessness and unrighteousness of people who by their unrighteousness suppress the truth, [19] since what can be known about God is evident among them, because God has shown it to them. [20] For his invisible attributes, that is, his eternal power and divine nature, have been clearly seen since the creation of the world, being understood through what he has made. As a result, people are without excuse. [21] For though they knew God, they did not glorify him as God or show gratitude. Instead, their thinking became worthless, and their senseless hearts were darkened. [22] Claiming to be wise, they became fools [23] and exchanged the glory of the immortal God for images resembling mortal man, birds, four-footed animals, and reptiles.

[24] Therefore God delivered them over in the desires of their hearts to sexual impurity, so that their bodies were degraded among themselves. [25] They exchanged the truth of God for a lie, and worshiped and served what has been created instead of the Creator, who is praised forever. Amen.

From Idolatry to Depravity

[26] For this reason God delivered them over to disgraceful passions. Their women exchanged natural sexual relations for unnatural ones. [27] The men in the same way also left natural relations with women and were inflamed in their lust for one another. Men committed shameless acts with men and received in their own persons the appropriate penalty of their error.

[28] And because they did not think it worthwhile to acknowledge God, God delivered them over to a corrupt mind so that they do what is not right. [29] They are filled with all unrighteousness, evil, greed, and wickedness. They are full of envy, murder, quarrels, deceit, and malice. They are gossips, [30] slanderers, God-haters, arrogant, proud, boastful, inventors of evil, disobedient to parents, [31] senseless, untrustworthy, unloving, and unmerciful. [32] Although they know God's just sentence—that those who practice such things deserve to die—they not only do them, but even applaud others who practice them.

TAKE ——————— NOTE

ISAIAH 44:9–11

[9] All who make idols are nothing,
and what they treasure benefits no one.
Their witnesses do not see or know anything,
so they will be put to shame.
[10] Who makes a god or casts a metal image
that benefits no one?
[11] Look, all its worshipers will be put to shame,
and the craftsmen are humans.
They all will assemble and stand;
they all will be startled and put to shame.

2 TIMOTHY 3:1–9

Difficult Times Ahead

[1] But know this: Hard times will come in the last days. [2] For people will be lovers of self, lovers of money, boastful, proud, demeaning, disobedient to parents, ungrateful, unholy, [3] unloving, irreconcilable, slanderers, without self-control, brutal, without love for what is good, [4] traitors, reckless, conceited, lovers of pleasure rather than lovers of God, [5] holding to the form of godliness but denying its power. Avoid these people.

[6] For among them are those who worm their way into households and deceive gullible women overwhelmed by sins and led astray by a variety of passions, [7] always learning and never able to come to a knowledge of the truth. [8] Just as Jannes and Jambres resisted Moses, so these also resist the truth. They are men who are corrupt in mind and worthless in regard to the faith. [9] But they will not make further progress, for their foolishness will be clear to all, as was the foolishness of Jannes and Jambres.

NOTES —————— DAY 02

They show that the work of the law is written on their hearts.   ROMANS 2:15

Faith in Action

ROMANS 2:1–16

God's Righteous Judgment

[1] Therefore, every one of you who judges is without excuse. For when you judge another, you condemn yourself, since you, the judge, do the same things. [2] Now we know that God's judgment on those who do such things is based on the truth. [3] Do you think—anyone of you who judges those who do such things yet do the same—that you will escape God's judgment? [4] Or do you despise the riches of his kindness, restraint, and patience, not recognizing that God's kindness is intended to lead you to repentance? [5] Because of your hardened and unrepentant heart you are storing up wrath for yourself in the day of wrath, when God's righteous judgment is revealed. [6] He will repay each one according to his works: [7] eternal life to those who by persistence in doing good seek glory, honor, and immortality; [8] but wrath and anger to those who are self-seeking and disobey the truth while obeying unrighteousness. [9] There will be affliction and distress for every human being who does evil, first to the Jew, and also to the Greek; [10] but glory, honor, and peace for everyone who does what is good, first to the Jew, and also to the Greek. [11] For there is no favoritism with God.

[12] For all who sin without the law will also perish without the law, and all who sin under the law will be judged by the law. [13] For the hearers of the law are not righteous before God, but the doers of the law will be justified. [14] So, when Gentiles, who do not by nature have the law, do what the law demands, they are a law to themselves even though they do not have the law. [15] They show that the work of the law is written on their hearts. Their consciences confirm this. Their competing thoughts either accuse or even excuse them [16] on the day when God judges what people have kept secret, according to my gospel through Christ Jesus.

♥ GOING DEEPER

PSALM 51:1–12

A Prayer for Restoration

For the choir director. A psalm of David, when the prophet Nathan came to him after he had gone to Bathsheba.

[1] Be gracious to me, God,
according to your faithful love;
according to your abundant compassion,
blot out my rebellion.
[2] Completely wash away my guilt
and cleanse me from my sin.
[3] For I am conscious of my rebellion,
and my sin is always before me.
[4] Against you—you alone—I have sinned
and done this evil in your sight.
So you are right when you pass sentence;
you are blameless when you judge.
[5] Indeed, I was guilty when I was born;
I was sinful when my mother conceived me.

[6] Surely you desire integrity in the inner self,
and you teach me wisdom deep within.
[7] Purify me with hyssop, and I will be clean;
wash me, and I will be whiter than snow.
[8] Let me hear joy and gladness;
let the bones you have crushed rejoice.
[9] Turn your face away from my sins
and blot out all my guilt.

[10] God, create a clean heart for me
and renew a steadfast spirit within me.
[11] Do not banish me from your presence
or take your Holy Spirit from me.
[12] Restore the joy of your salvation to me,
and sustain me by giving me a willing spirit.

JAMES 1:22–25

[22] But be doers of the word and not hearers only, deceiving yourselves. [23] Because if anyone is a hearer of the word and not a doer, he is like someone looking at his own face in a mirror. [24] For he looks at himself, goes away, and immediately forgets what kind of person he was. [25] But the one who looks intently into the perfect law of freedom and perseveres in it, and is not a forgetful hearer but a doer who works—this person will be blessed in what he does.

NOTES ———— DAY 03

True

DAY

04

Obedience

ROMANS 2:17–29

Jewish Violation of the Law

[17] Now if you call yourself a Jew, and rely on the law, and boast in God, [18] and know his will, and approve the things that are superior, being instructed from the law, [19] and if you are convinced that you are a guide for the blind, a light to those in darkness, [20] an instructor of the ignorant, a teacher of the immature, having the embodiment of knowledge and truth in the law— [21] you then, who teach another, don't you teach yourself? You who preach, "You must not steal"—do you steal? [22] You who say, "You must not commit adultery"—do you commit adultery? You who detest idols, do you rob temples? [23] You who boast in the law, do you dishonor God by breaking the law? [24] For, as it is written: The name of God is blasphemed among the Gentiles because of you.

Circumcision of the Heart

[25] Circumcision benefits you if you observe the law, but if you are a lawbreaker, your circumcision has become uncircumcision. [26] So if an uncircumcised man keeps the law's requirements, will not his uncircumcision be counted as circumcision? [27] A man who is physically uncircumcised, but who keeps the law, will judge you who are a lawbreaker in spite of having the letter of the law and circumcision. [28] For a person is not a Jew who is one outwardly, and true circumcision is not something visible in the flesh. [29] On the contrary, a person is a Jew who is one inwardly, and circumcision is of the heart—by the Spirit, not the letter. That person's praise is not from people but from God.

♥ GOING DEEPER

DEUTERONOMY 10:12–17

What God Requires

[12] And now, Israel, what does the LORD your God ask of you except to fear the LORD your God by walking in all his ways, to love him, and to worship the LORD your God with all your heart and all your soul? [13] Keep the LORD's commands and statutes I am giving you today, for your own good. [14] The heavens, indeed the highest heavens, belong to the LORD your God, as does the earth and everything in it.

[15] Yet the Lord had his heart set on your ancestors and loved them. He chose their descendants after them—he chose you out of all the peoples, as it is today. [16] Therefore, circumcise your hearts and don't be stiff-necked any longer. [17] For the Lord your God is the God of gods and Lord of lords, the great, mighty, and awe-inspiring God, showing no partiality and taking no bribe.

MATTHEW 23:1–7

Religious Hypocrites Denounced

[1] Then Jesus spoke to the crowds and to his disciples: [2] "The scribes and the Pharisees are seated in the chair of Moses. [3] Therefore do whatever they tell you, and observe it. But don't do what they do, because they don't practice what they teach. [4] They tie up heavy loads that are hard to carry and put them on people's shoulders, but they themselves aren't willing to lift a finger to move them. [5] They do everything to be seen by others: They enlarge their phylacteries and lengthen their tassels. [6] They love the place of honor at banquets, the front seats in the synagogues, [7] greetings in the marketplaces, and to be called 'Rabbi' by people."

No One

Is Righteous

ROMANS 3:1–20

Paul Answers an Objection

¹ So what advantage does the Jew have? Or what is the benefit of circumcision? ² Considerable in every way. First, they were entrusted with the very words of God. ³ What then? If some were unfaithful, will their unfaithfulness nullify God's faithfulness? ⁴ Absolutely not! Let God be true, even though everyone is a liar, as it is written:

> That you may be justified in your words
> and triumph when you judge.

⁵ But if our unrighteousness highlights God's righteousness, what are we to say? I am using a human argument: Is God unrighteous to inflict wrath? ⁶ Absolutely not! Otherwise, how will God judge the world? ⁷ But if by my lie God's truth abounds to his glory, why am I also still being judged as a sinner? ⁸ And why not say, just as some people slanderously claim we say, "Let us do what is evil so that good may come"? Their condemnation is deserved!

The Whole World Guilty Before God

⁹ What then? Are we any better off? Not at all! For we have already charged that both Jews and Greeks are all under sin, ¹⁰ as it is written:

There is no one righteous, not even one.
¹¹ There is no one who understands;
there is no one who seeks God.
¹² All have turned away;
all alike have become worthless.
There is no one who does what is good,
not even one.
¹³ Their throat is an open grave;
they deceive with their tongues.
Vipers' venom is under their lips.
¹⁴ Their mouth is full of cursing and bitterness.
¹⁵ Their feet are swift to shed blood;
¹⁶ ruin and wretchedness are in their paths,
¹⁷ and the path of peace they have not known.
¹⁸ There is no fear of God before their eyes.

¹⁹ Now we know that whatever the law says, it speaks to those who are subject to the law, so that every mouth may be shut and the whole world may become subject to God's judgment. ²⁰ For no one will be justified in his sight by the works of the law, because the knowledge of sin comes through the law.

ECCLESIASTES 7:20

There is certainly no one
righteous on the earth
who does good and never sins.

GALATIANS 3:22

But the Scripture imprisoned everything under sin's power, so that the promise might be given on the basis of faith in Jesus Christ to those who believe.

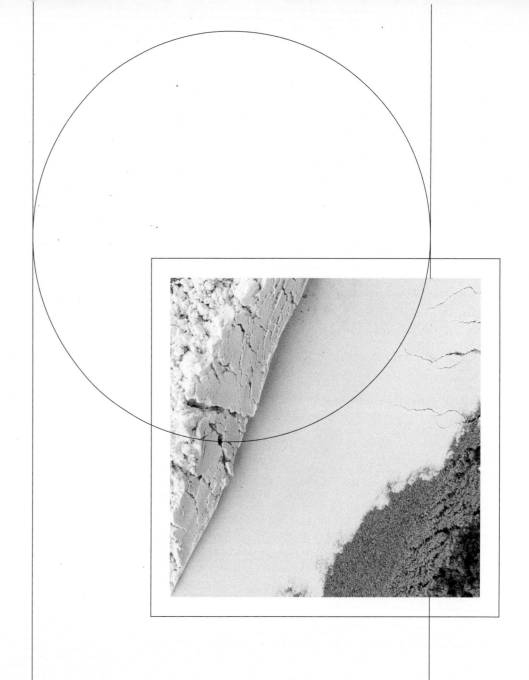

Response

Use the following questions each week to reflect on your reading from the book of Romans. Themes may stand out to you more in some weeks than others—you may not have an answer for each question every week, and that's okay! These questions are a guide for you to ground yourself in reflecting on the letter to the Romans and your weekly reading as a whole.

01

Paul's longing for the people of Rome to better understand the truth of the gospel?

02

passages intended to address division or tension?

03

instructions for believers to represent Christ faithfully in their everyday lives?

Take this day to catch up on your reading, pray, and rest in the presence of the Lord.

Surely you desire integrity in the inner self, and you teach me wisdom deep within.

PSALM 51:6

Weekly

DAY ——————————

Scripture is God-breathed and true. When we memorize it, we carry the good news of Jesus with us wherever we go.

For this reading plan, we will memorize Romans 3:22–24, which is a reminder that, though we are sinners who have fallen short, we are given access to God's righteousness when we believe and trust in Christ for His redemption. We'll start by memorizing the first portion of verse 22.

SEE TIPS FOR MEMORIZING SCRIPTURE ON PAGE (164.)

Truth

ROMANS 3:22–24

²² <u>The righteousness of God is through faith in Jesus Christ to all who believe,</u> since there is no distinction. ²³ For all have sinned and fall short of the glory of God; ²⁴ they are justified freely by his grace through the redemption that is in Christ Jesus.

Faith in

Jesus Christ

ROMANS 3:21–31

The Righteousness of God Through Faith

[21] But now, apart from the law, the righteousness of God has been revealed, attested by the Law and the Prophets. [22] The righteousness of God is through faith in Jesus Christ to all who believe, since there is no distinction. [23] For all have sinned and fall short of the glory of God; [24] they are justified freely by his grace through the redemption that is in Christ Jesus. [25] God presented him as the mercy seat by his blood, through faith, to demonstrate his righteousness, because in his restraint God passed over the sins previously committed. [26] God presented him to demonstrate his righteousness at the present time, so that he would be just and justify the one who has faith in Jesus.

Boasting Excluded

[27] Where, then, is boasting? It is excluded. By what kind of law? By one of works? No, on the contrary, by a law of faith.

> [28] For we conclude that a person is justified by faith apart from the works of the law.

[29] Or is God the God of Jews only? Is he not the God of Gentiles too? Yes, of Gentiles too, [30] since there is one God who will justify the circumcised by faith and the uncircumcised through faith. [31] Do we then nullify the law through faith? Absolutely not! On the contrary, we uphold the law.

■ GOING DEEPER

ACTS 10:28–43

[28] Peter said to them, "You know it's forbidden for a Jewish man to associate with or visit a foreigner, but God has shown me that I must not call any person impure or unclean. [29] That's why I came without any objection when I was sent for. So may I ask why you sent for me?"

[30] Cornelius replied, "Four days ago at this hour, at three in the afternoon, I was praying in my house. Just then a man in dazzling clothing stood before me [31] and said, 'Cornelius, your prayer has been heard, and your acts of charity have

been remembered in God's sight. ³² Therefore send someone to Joppa and invite Simon here, who is also named Peter. He is lodging in Simon the tanner's house by the sea.' ³³ So I immediately sent for you, and it was good of you to come. So now we are all in the presence of God to hear everything you have been commanded by the Lord."

Good News for Gentiles

³⁴ Peter began to speak: "Now I truly understand that God doesn't show favoritism, ³⁵ but in every nation the person who fears him and does what is right is acceptable to him. ³⁶ He sent the message to the Israelites, proclaiming the good news of peace through Jesus Christ—he is Lord of all. ³⁷ You know the events that took place throughout all Judea, beginning from Galilee after the baptism that John preached: ³⁸ how God anointed Jesus of Nazareth with the Holy Spirit and with power, and how he went about doing good and healing all who were under the tyranny of the devil, because God was with him. ³⁹ We ourselves are witnesses of everything he did in both the Judean country and in Jerusalem, and yet they killed him by hanging him on a tree. ⁴⁰ God raised up this man on the third day and caused him to be seen, ⁴¹ not by all the people, but by us whom God appointed as witnesses, who ate and drank with him after he rose from the dead. ⁴² He commanded us to preach to the people and to testify that he is the one appointed by God to be the judge of the living and the dead. ⁴³ All the prophets testify about him that through his name everyone who believes in him receives forgiveness of sins."

COLOSSIANS 1:13–14

¹³ He has rescued us from the domain of darkness and transferred us into the kingdom of the Son he loves. ¹⁴ In him we have redemption, the forgiveness of sins.

NOTES

A Map of Paul's Travels

In Acts 1:8, Jesus told His apostles to share the gospel with people "in Jerusalem, in all Judea and Samaria, and to the ends of the earth." His followers began to carry out His instructions, starting after Pentecost (Ac 2). Paul and his fellow coworkers in the gospel were the first to undertake the mission of traveling and sharing the gospel, encouraging churches as their numbers grew (Ac 18:19–21).

Paul was faithful to reach Jerusalem, Judea, and Samaria and considered himself to "no longer have any work to do in these regions" (Rm 15:23). His next step was to embark on a journey to share the gospel with the "ends of the earth." For Paul, that meant launching a trip to Spain, which was located in the western Roman Empire. While we don't know whether or not Paul made it to Spain, Rome was a key city Paul planned to stop at on his way there.

Turn the page for a map that shows the routes Paul traveled on his various missionary journeys in relation to Jerusalem, Judea, Samaria, and other places he desired to visit.

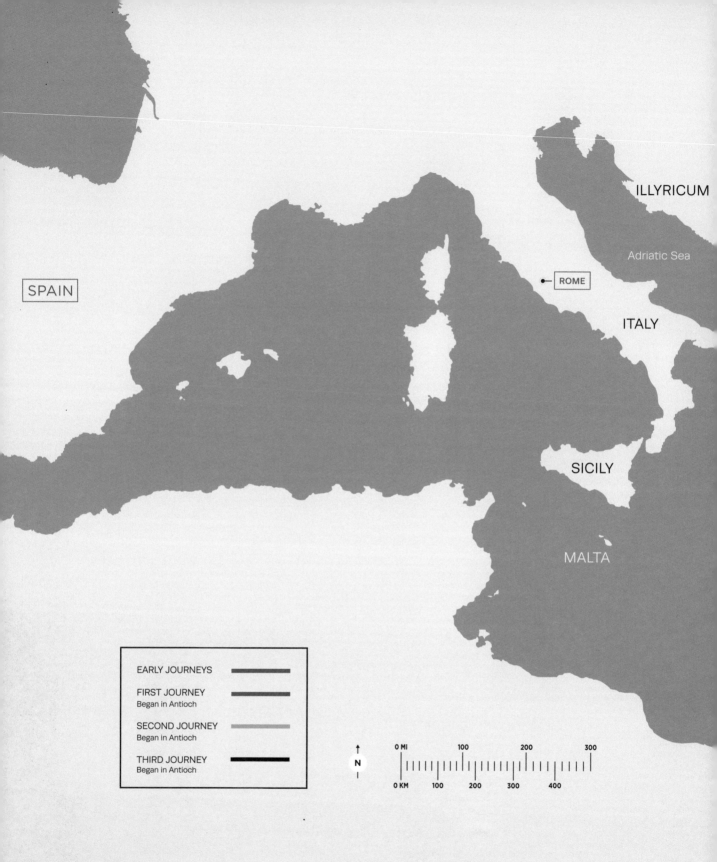

SPAIN

ILLYRICUM

Adriatic Sea

ROME

ITALY

SICILY

MALTA

EARLY JOURNEYS

FIRST JOURNEY
Began in Antioch

SECOND JOURNEY
Began in Antioch

THIRD JOURNEY
Began in Antioch

N

0 MI   100   200   300

0 KM   100   200   300   400

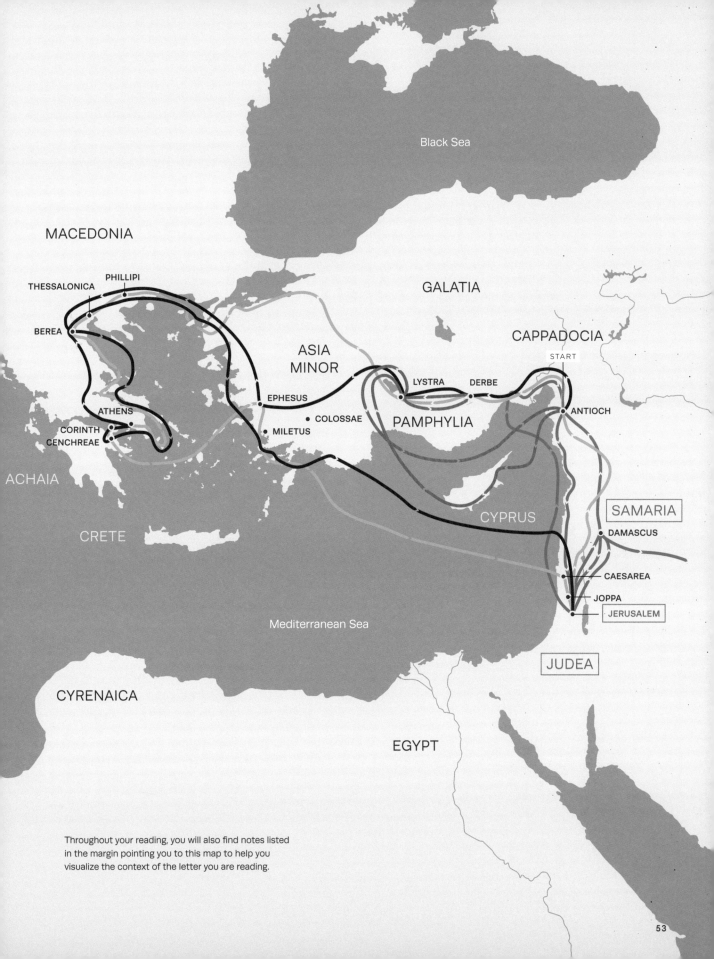

Black Sea

MACEDONIA

GALATIA

THESSALONICA

PHILLIPI

CAPPADOCIA

BEREA

ASIA
MINOR

START

LYSTRA   DERBE

ATHENS

EPHESUS

ANTIOCH

CORINTH

COLOSSAE

PAMPHYLIA

CENCHREAE

MILETUS

ACHAIA

CYPRUS

SAMARIA

CRETE

DAMASCUS

CAESAREA

Mediterranean Sea

JOPPA

JERUSALEM

JUDEA

CYRENAICA

EGYPT

Throughout your reading, you will also find notes listed
in the margin pointing you to this map to help you
visualize the context of the letter you are reading.

The Promise Granted Through Faith

He was delivered
up for our trespasses
and raised for
our justification.

ROMANS 4:25

ROMANS 4

Abraham Justified by Faith

[1] What then will we say that Abraham, our forefather according to the flesh, has found? [2] If Abraham was justified by works, he has something to boast about—but not before God. [3] For what does the Scripture say? Abraham believed God, and it was credited to him for righteousness. [4] Now to the one who works, pay is not credited as a gift, but as something owed. [5] But to the one who does not work, but believes on him who justifies the ungodly, his faith is credited for righteousness.

David Celebrating the Same Truth

[6] Likewise, David also speaks of the blessing of the person to whom God credits righteousness apart from works:

[7] Blessed are those whose lawless acts are forgiven
and whose sins are covered.
[8] Blessed is the person
the Lord will never charge with sin.

Abraham Justified Before Circumcision

[9] Is this blessing only for the circumcised, then? Or is it also for the uncircumcised? For we say, Faith was credited to Abraham for righteousness. [10] In what way, then, was it credited—while he was circumcised, or uncircumcised? It was not while he was circumcised, but uncircumcised. [11] And he received the sign of circumcision as a seal of the righteousness that he had by faith while still uncircumcised. This was to make him the father of all who believe but are not circumcised, so that righteousness may be credited to them also. [12] And he became the father of the circumcised, who are not only circumcised but who also follow in the footsteps of the faith our father Abraham had while still uncircumcised.

The Promise Granted Through Faith

[13] For the promise to Abraham or to his descendants that he would inherit the world was not through the law, but through the righteousness that comes by faith. [14] If those who are of the law are heirs, faith is made empty and the promise nullified, [15] because the law produces wrath. And where there is no law, there is no transgression.

[16] This is why the promise is by faith, so that it may be according to grace, to guarantee it to all the descendants—

not only to the one who is of the law but also to the one who is of Abraham's faith. He is the father of us all. [17] As it is written: I have made you the father of many nations—in the presence of the God in whom he believed, the one who gives life to the dead and calls things into existence that do not exist. [18] He believed, hoping against hope, so that he became the father of many nations according to what had been spoken: So will your descendants be. [19] He did not weaken in faith when he considered his own body to be already dead (since he was about a hundred years old) and also the deadness of Sarah's womb. [20] He did not waver in unbelief at God's promise but was strengthened in his faith and gave glory to God, [21] because he was fully convinced that what God had promised, he was also able to do. [22] Therefore, it was credited to him for righteousness. [23] Now it was credited to him was not written for Abraham alone, [24] but also for us. It will be credited to us who believe in him who raised Jesus our Lord from the dead. [25] He was delivered up for our trespasses and raised for our justification.

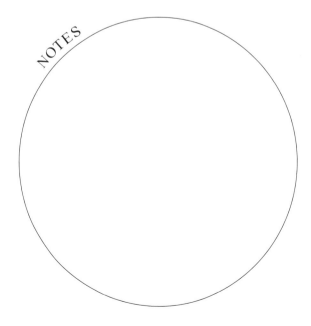

GOING DEEPER

PSALM 32:1–2

The Joy of Forgiveness
Of David. A Maskil.

[1] How joyful is the one
whose transgression is forgiven,
whose sin is covered!
[2] How joyful is a person whom
the LORD does not charge with iniquity
and in whose spirit is no deceit!

EPHESIANS 2:4–7

[4] But God, who is rich in mercy, because of his great love that he had for us, [5] made us alive with Christ even though we were dead in trespasses. You are saved by grace! [6] He also raised us up with him and seated us with him in the heavens in Christ Jesus, [7] so that in the coming ages he might display the immeasurable riches of his grace through his kindness to us in Christ Jesus.

NOTES —————— DAY 09

57

We have peace with God through our Lord Jesus Christ.

Peace with God

ROMANS 5:1–11

Faith Triumphs

[1] Therefore, since we have been justified by faith, we have peace with God through our Lord Jesus Christ. [2] We have also obtained access through him by faith into this grace in which we stand, and we boast in the hope of the glory of God. [3] And not only that, but we also boast in our afflictions, because we know that affliction produces endurance, [4] endurance produces proven character, and proven character produces hope. [5] This hope will not disappoint us, because God's love has been poured out in our hearts through the Holy Spirit who was given to us.

The Justified Are Reconciled

[6] For while we were still helpless, at the right time, Christ died for the ungodly. [7] For rarely will someone die for a just person—though for a good person perhaps someone might even dare to die. [8] But God proves his own love for us in that while we were still sinners, Christ died for us. [9] How much more then, since we have now been justified by his blood, will we be saved through him from wrath. [10] For if, while we were enemies, we were reconciled to God through the death of his Son, then how much more, having been reconciled, will we be saved by his life. [11] And not only that, but we also boast in God through our Lord Jesus Christ, through whom we have now received this reconciliation.

♥ GOING DEEPER

ISAIAH 57:14–19

Healing and Peace

[14] He said,

"Build it up, build it up, prepare the way,
remove every obstacle from my people's way."
[15] For the High and Exalted One,
who lives forever, whose name is holy, says this:
"I live in a high and holy place,
and with the oppressed and lowly of spirit,
to revive the spirit of the lowly
and revive the heart of the oppressed.
[16] For I will not accuse you forever,
and I will not always be angry;

for then the spirit would grow weak before me,
even the breath, which I have made.
[17] Because of his sinful greed I was angry,
so I struck him; I was angry and hid;
but he went on turning back to the desires of his heart.
[18] I have seen his ways, but I will heal him;
I will lead him and restore comfort
to him and his mourners,
[19] creating words of praise."
The LORD says,
"Peace, peace to the one who is far or near,
and I will heal him."

EPHESIANS 2:11–22

Unity in Christ

[11] So, then, remember that at one time you were Gentiles in the flesh—called "the uncircumcised" by those called "the circumcised," which is done in the flesh by human hands. [12] At that time you were without Christ, excluded from the citizenship of Israel, and foreigners to the covenants of promise, without hope and without God in the world. [13] But now in Christ Jesus, you who were far away have been brought near by the blood of Christ. [14] For he is our peace, who made both groups one and tore down the dividing wall of hostility. In his flesh, [15] he made of no effect the law consisting of commands and expressed in regulations, so that he might create in himself one new man from the two, resulting in peace. [16] He did this so that he might reconcile both to God in one body through the cross by which he put the hostility to death. [17] He came and proclaimed the good news of peace to you who were far away and peace to those who were near. [18] For through him we both have access in one Spirit to the Father. [19] So, then, you are no longer foreigners and strangers, but fellow citizens with the saints, and members of God's household, [20] built on the foundation of the apostles and prophets, with Christ Jesus himself as the cornerstone. [21] In him the whole building, being put together, grows into a holy temple in the Lord. [22] In him you are also being built together for God's dwelling in the Spirit.

NOTES ———— DAY 10

Death Through Adam

DAY —————————— 11

and Life Through Christ

ROMANS 5:12–21

Death Through Adam and Life Through Christ

12 Therefore, just as sin entered the world through one man, and death through sin, in this way death spread to all people, because all sinned. 13 In fact, sin was in the world before the law, but sin is not charged to a person's account when there is no law. 14 Nevertheless, death reigned from Adam to Moses, even over those who did not sin in the likeness of Adam's transgression. He is a type of the Coming One.

15 But the gift is not like the trespass. For if by the one man's trespass the many died, how much more have the grace of God and the gift which comes through the grace of the one man Jesus Christ overflowed to the many. 16 And the gift is not like the one man's sin, because from one sin came the judgment, resulting in condemnation, but from many trespasses came the gift, resulting in justification. 17 If by the one man's trespass, death reigned through that one man, how much more will those who receive the overflow of grace and the gift of righteousness reign in life through the one man, Jesus Christ.

18 So then, as through one trespass there is condemnation for everyone, so also through one righteous act there is justification leading to life for everyone. 19 For just as through one man's disobedience the many were made sinners, so also through the one man's obedience the many will be made righteous. 20 The law came along to multiply the trespass. But where sin multiplied, grace multiplied even more 21 so that, just as sin reigned in death, so also grace will reign through righteousness, resulting in eternal life through Jesus Christ our Lord.

GENESIS 3:17–19

[17] And he said to the man, "Because you listened to your wife and ate from the tree about which I commanded you, 'Do not eat from it':

The ground is cursed because of you.
You will eat from it by means of painful labor
all the days of your life.
[18] It will produce thorns and thistles for you,
and you will eat the plants of the field.
[19] You will eat bread by the sweat of your brow
until you return to the ground,
since you were taken from it.
For you are dust,
and you will return to dust."

1 CORINTHIANS 15:21–22

[21] For since death came through a man, the resurrection of the dead also comes through a man. [22] For just as in Adam all die, so also in Christ all will be made alive.

The New Life

DAY 12

in Christ

ROMANS 6:1–14

The New Life in Christ

[1] What should we say then? Should we continue in sin so that grace may multiply? [2] Absolutely not! How can we who died to sin still live in it? [3] Or are you unaware that all of us who were baptized into Christ Jesus were baptized into his death? [4] Therefore we were buried with him by baptism into death, in order that, just as Christ was raised from the dead by the glory of the Father, so we too may walk in newness of life. [5] For if we have been united with him in the likeness of his death, we will certainly also be in the likeness of his resurrection. [6] For we know that our old self was crucified with him so that the body ruled by sin might be rendered powerless so that we may no longer be enslaved to sin, [7] since a person who has died is freed from sin. [8] Now if we died with Christ, we believe that we will also live with him, [9] because we know that Christ, having been raised from the dead, will not die again. Death no longer rules over him. [10] For the death he died, he died to sin once for all time; but the life he lives, he lives to God. [11] So, you too consider yourselves dead to sin and alive to God in Christ Jesus.

[12] Therefore do not let sin reign in your mortal body, so that you obey its desires. [13] And do not offer any parts of it to sin as weapons for unrighteousness. But as those who are alive from the dead, offer yourselves to God, and all the parts of yourselves to God as weapons for righteousness. [14] For sin will not rule over you, because you are not under the law but under grace.

❤ GOING DEEPER

2 CORINTHIANS 5:17–21

> [17] Therefore, if anyone is in Christ, he is a new creation; the old has passed away, and see, the new has come!

[18] Everything is from God, who has reconciled us to himself through Christ and has given us the ministry of reconciliation. [19] That is, in Christ, God was reconciling the world to himself, not counting their trespasses against them, and he has committed the message of reconciliation to us.

[20] Therefore, we are ambassadors for Christ, since God is making his appeal through us. We plead on Christ's behalf, "Be reconciled to God." [21] He made the one who did not know sin to be sin for us, so that in him we might become the righteousness of God.

COLOSSIANS 3:2–11

[2] Set your minds on things above, not on earthly things. [3] For you died, and your life is hidden with Christ in God. [4] When Christ, who is your life, appears, then you also will appear with him in glory.

[5] Therefore, put to death what belongs to your earthly nature: sexual immorality, impurity, lust, evil desire, and greed, which is idolatry. [6] Because of these, God's wrath is coming upon the disobedient, [7] and you once walked in these things when you were living in them. [8] But now, put away all the following: anger, wrath, malice, slander, and filthy language from your mouth. [9] Do not lie to one another, since you have put off the old self with its practices [10] and have put on the new self. You are being renewed in knowledge according to the image of your Creator. [11] In Christ there is not Greek and Jew, circumcision and uncircumcision, barbarian, Scythian, slave and free; but Christ is all and in all.

NOTES ———————————— DAY 12

Response

01

Paul's longing for the people of Rome to better understand the truth of the gospel?

02

passages intended to address division or tension?

03

instructions for believers to represent Christ faithfully in their everyday lives?

Take this day to catch up on your reading,
pray, and rest in the presence of the Lord.

But now in Christ
Jesus, you who were
far away have been
brought near by the
blood of Christ.

EPHESIANS 2:13

Weekly

Scripture is God-breathed and true. When we memorize it, we carry the good news of Jesus with us wherever we go.

For this reading plan, we are memorizing Romans 3:22–24. This week we'll add the remainder of verse 22, a declaration that there are no distinctions among believers.

SEE TIPS FOR MEMORIZING SCRIPTURE ON PAGE 164.

Truth

ROMANS 3:22–24

²² The righteousness of God is through faith in Jesus Christ to all who believe, <u>since there is no distinction.</u> ²³ For all have sinned and fall short of the glory of God; ²⁴ they are justified freely by his grace through the redemption that is in Christ Jesus.

Belong to God

DAY —————————————————————— 15

Having been set free from sin, you
became enslaved to righteousness.

ROMANS 6:18

ROMANS 6:15–23

From Slaves of Sin to Slaves of God

[15] What then? Should we sin because we are not under the law but under grace? Absolutely not! [16] Don't you know that if you offer yourselves to someone as obedient slaves, you are slaves of that one you obey—either of sin leading to death or of obedience leading to righteousness? [17] But thank God that, although you used to be slaves of sin, you obeyed from the heart that pattern of teaching to which you were handed over, [18] and having been set free from sin, you became enslaved to righteousness. [19] I am using a human analogy because of the weakness of your flesh.

> For just as you offered the parts of yourselves as slaves to impurity, and to greater and greater lawlessness, so now offer them as slaves to righteousness, which results in sanctification.

[20] For when you were slaves of sin, you were free with regard to righteousness. [21] So what fruit was produced then from the things you are now ashamed of? The outcome of those things is death. [22] But now, since you have been set free from sin and have become enslaved to God, you have your fruit, which results in sanctification—and the outcome is eternal life! [23] For the wages of sin is death, but the gift of God is eternal life in Christ Jesus our Lord.

◆ GOING DEEPER

ISAIAH 61

Messiah's Jubilee

[1] The Spirit of the Lord GOD is on me, because the LORD has anointed me to bring good news to the poor. He has sent me to heal the brokenhearted, to proclaim liberty to the captives and freedom to the prisoners; [2] to proclaim the year of the LORD's favor, and the day of our God's vengeance; to comfort all who mourn,

[3] to provide for those who mourn in Zion; to give them a crown of beauty instead of ashes, festive oil instead of mourning, and splendid clothes instead of despair. And they will be called righteous trees, planted by the LORD to glorify him. [4] They will rebuild the ancient ruins; they will restore the former devastations; they will renew the ruined cities, the devastations of many generations. [5] Strangers will stand and feed your flocks, and foreigners will be your plowmen and vinedressers.

[6] But you will be called the LORD's priests; they will speak of you as ministers of our God; you will eat the wealth of the nations, and you will boast in their riches. [7] In place of your shame, you will have a double portion; in place of disgrace, they will rejoice over their share. So they will possess double in their land, and eternal joy will be theirs.

[8] For I the LORD love justice; I hate robbery and injustice; I will faithfully reward my people and make a permanent covenant with them. [9] Their descendants will be known among the nations, and their posterity among the peoples. All who see them will recognize that they are a people the LORD has blessed.

[10] I rejoice greatly in the LORD, I exult in my God; for he has clothed me with the garments of salvation and wrapped me in a robe of righteousness, as a groom wears a turban and as a bride adorns herself with her jewels. [11] For as the earth produces its growth, and as a garden enables what is sown to spring up, so the Lord GOD will cause righteousness and praise to spring up before all the nations.

GALATIANS 5:1, 13–14

Freedom of the Christian

[1] For freedom, Christ set us free. Stand firm, then, and don't submit again to a yoke of slavery.

…

[13] For you were called to be free, brothers and sisters; only don't use this freedom as an opportunity for the flesh,

but serve one another through love. [14] For the whole law is fulfilled in one statement: Love your neighbor as yourself.

NOTES

The Problem

# of Sin in Us

ROMANS 7

An Illustration from Marriage

[1] Since I am speaking to those who know the law, brothers and sisters, don't you know that the law rules over someone as long as he lives? [2] For example, a married woman is legally bound to her husband while he lives. But if her husband dies, she is released from the law regarding the husband. [3] So then, if she is married to another man while her husband is living, she will be called an adulteress. But if her husband dies, she is free from that law. Then, if she is married to another man, she is not an adulteress.

[4] Therefore, my brothers and sisters, you also were put to death in relation to the law through the body of Christ so that you may belong to another. You belong to him who was raised from the dead in order that we may bear fruit for God. [5] For when we were in the flesh, the sinful passions aroused through the law were working in us to bear fruit for death. [6] But now we have been released from the law, since we have died to what held us, so that we may serve in the newness of the Spirit and not in the old letter of the law.

Sin's Use of the Law

[7] What should we say then? Is the law sin? Absolutely not! But I would not have known sin if it were not for the law. For example, I would not have known what it is to covet if the law had not said, Do not covet. [8] And sin, seizing an opportunity through the commandment, produced in me coveting of every kind. For apart from the law sin is dead. [9] Once I was alive apart from the law, but when the commandment came, sin sprang to life again [10] and I died. The commandment that was meant for life resulted in death for me. [11] For sin, seizing an opportunity through the commandment, deceived me, and through it killed me. [12] So then, the law is holy, and the commandment is holy and just and good. [13] Therefore, did what is good become death to me? Absolutely not! But sin, in order to be recognized as sin, was producing death in me through what is good, so that through the commandment, sin might become sinful beyond measure.

The Problem of Sin in Us

[14] For we know that the law is spiritual, but I am of the flesh, sold as a slave under sin. [15] For I do not understand what I

am doing, because I do not practice what I want to do, but I do what I hate. ¹⁶ Now if I do what I do not want to do, I agree with the law that it is good. ¹⁷ So now I am no longer the one doing it, but it is sin living in me. ¹⁸ For I know that nothing good lives in me, that is, in my flesh. For the desire to do what is good is with me, but there is no ability to do it. ¹⁹ For I do not do the good that I want to do, but I practice the evil that I do not want to do. ²⁰ Now if I do what I do not want, I am no longer the one that does it, but it is the sin that lives in me. ²¹ So I discover this law: When I want to do what is good, evil is present with me. ²² For in my inner self I delight in God's law, ²³ but I see a different law in the parts of my body, waging war against the law of my mind and taking me prisoner to the law of sin in the parts of my body. ²⁴ What a wretched man I am! Who will rescue me from this body of death? ²⁵ Thanks be to God through Jesus Christ our Lord! So then, with my mind I myself am serving the law of God, but with my flesh, the law of sin.

♥ GOING DEEPER

PSALM 53:1–3

A Portrait of Sinners

For the choir director: on Mahalath. *A Maskil of David.*

¹ The fool says in his heart, "There's no God."
They are corrupt, and they do vile deeds.
There is no one who does good.
² God looks down from heaven on the human race
to see if there is one who is wise,
one who seeks God.
³ All have turned away;
all alike have become corrupt.
There is no one who does good,
not even one.

GALATIANS 5:16–26

The Spirit Versus the Flesh

¹⁶ I say, then, walk by the Spirit and you will certainly not carry out the desire of the flesh.

> ¹⁷ For the flesh desires what is against the Spirit, and the Spirit desires what is against the flesh; these are opposed to each other, so that you don't do what you want. ¹⁸ But if you are led by the Spirit, you are not under the law.

¹⁹ Now the works of the flesh are obvious: sexual immorality, moral impurity, promiscuity, ²⁰ idolatry, sorcery, hatreds, strife, jealousy, outbursts of anger, selfish ambitions, dissensions, factions, ²¹ envy, drunkenness, carousing, and anything similar. I am warning you about these things—as I warned you before—that those who practice such things will not inherit the kingdom of God.

²² But the fruit of the Spirit is love, joy, peace, patience, kindness, goodness, faithfulness, ²³ gentleness, and self-control. The law is not against such things. ²⁴ Now those who belong to Christ Jesus have crucified the flesh with its passions and desires. ²⁵ If we live by the Spirit, let us also keep in step with the Spirit. ²⁶ Let us not become conceited, provoking one another, envying one another.

NOTES ——————— DAY 16

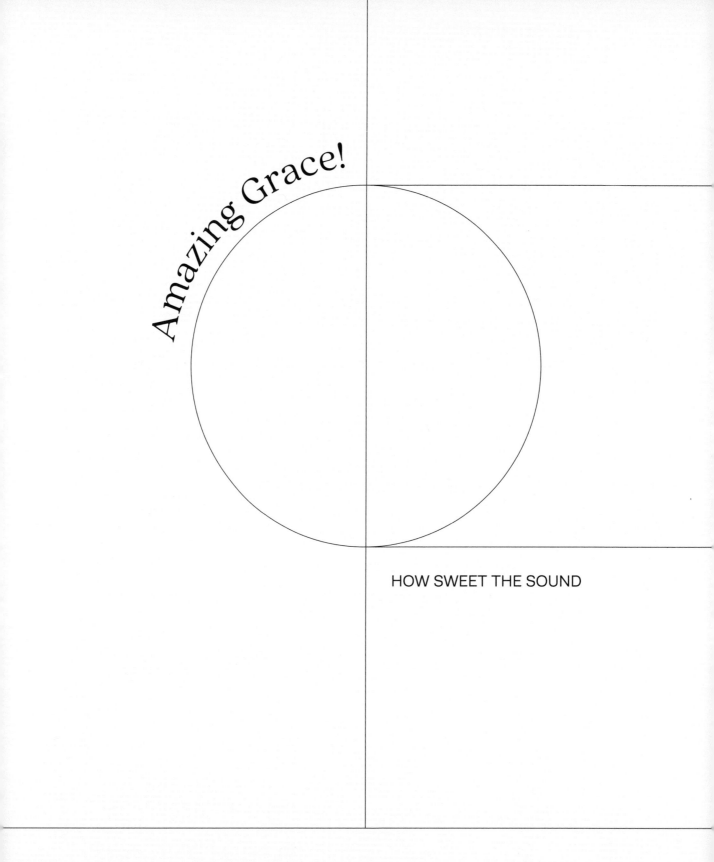

Amazing Grace!

HOW SWEET THE SOUND

1. A - maz - ing grace! how sweet the sound that saved a wretch like me!
2. 'Twas grace that taught my heart to fear, And grace my fears re - lieved;
3. Through man - y dan - gers, toils and snares I have al - read - y come;
4. The Lord has prom - ised good to me, His word my hope se - cures;
5. When we've been there ten thou - sand years, Bright shin - ing as the sun,

I once was lost but now am found, Was blind, but now I see.
How pre - cious did that grace ap - pear the hour I first be - lieved!
'Tis grace hath brought me safe thus far, And grace will lead me home.
He will my shield and por - tion be as long as life en - dures.
We've no less days to sing God's praise than when we first be - gun.

WORDS: John Newton; fifth stanza by John P. Rees
MUSIC: *Virginia Harmony*; arrangement by Edwin O. Excell

The Life-Giving Spirit

The law of the Spirit of
life in Christ Jesus has
set you free from the
law of sin and death.

ROMANS 8:2

ROMANS 8:1–17

The Life-Giving Spirit

[1] Therefore, there is now no condemnation for those in Christ Jesus, [2] because the law of the Spirit of life in Christ Jesus has set you free from the law of sin and death. [3] For what the law could not do since it was weakened by the flesh, God did. He condemned sin in the flesh by sending his own Son in the likeness of sinful flesh as a sin offering, [4] in order that the law's requirement would be fulfilled in us who do not walk according to the flesh but according to the Spirit. [5] For those who live according to the flesh have their minds set on the things of the flesh, but those who live according to the Spirit have their minds set on the things of the Spirit. [6] Now the mindset of the flesh is death, but the mindset of the Spirit is life and peace. [7] The mindset of the flesh is hostile to God because it does not submit to God's law. Indeed, it is unable to do so. [8] Those who are in the flesh cannot please God. [9] You, however, are not in the flesh, but in the Spirit, if indeed the Spirit of God lives in you. If anyone does not have the Spirit of Christ, he does not belong to him.

> [10] Now if Christ is in you, the body is dead because of sin, but the Spirit gives life because of righteousness. [11] And if the Spirit of him who raised Jesus from the dead lives in you, then he who raised Christ from the dead will also bring your mortal bodies to life through his Spirit who lives in you.

The Holy Spirit's Ministries

[12] So then, brothers and sisters, we are not obligated to the flesh to live according to the flesh, [13] because if you live according to the flesh, you are going to die. But if by the Spirit you put to death the deeds of the body, you will live. [14] For all those led by God's Spirit are God's sons. [15] For you did not receive a spirit of slavery to fall back into fear. Instead, you received the Spirit of adoption, by whom we cry out, *"Abba*, Father!" [16] The Spirit himself testifies together with our spirit that we are God's children, [17] and if children, also heirs—heirs of God and coheirs with Christ—if indeed we suffer with him so that we may also be glorified with him.

⬟ GOING DEEPER

EZEKIEL 36:24–30

[24] "For I will take you from the nations and gather you from all the countries, and will bring you into your own land. [25] I will also sprinkle clean water on you, and you will be clean. I will cleanse you from all your impurities and all your idols. [26] I will give you a new heart and put a new spirit within you; I will remove your heart of stone and give you a heart of flesh. [27] I will place my Spirit within you and cause you to follow my statutes and carefully observe my ordinances. [28] You will live in the land that I gave your ancestors; you will be my people, and I will be your God. [29] I will save you from all your uncleanness. I will summon the grain and make it plentiful, and I will not bring famine on you. [30] I will also make the fruit of the trees and the produce of the field plentiful, so that you will no longer experience reproach among the nations on account of famine."

JOHN 16:1–15

[1] "I have told you these things to keep you from stumbling. [2] They will ban you from the synagogues. In fact, a time is coming when anyone who kills you will think he is offering

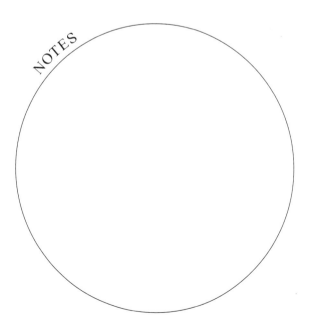

NOTES

service to God. ³ They will do these things because they haven't known the Father or me. ⁴ But I have told you these things so that when their time comes you will remember I told them to you. I didn't tell you these things from the beginning, because I was with you. ⁵ But now I am going away to him who sent me, and not one of you asks me, 'Where are you going?' ⁶ Yet, because I have spoken these things to you, sorrow has filled your heart. ⁷ Nevertheless, I am telling you the truth. It is for your benefit that I go away, because if I don't go away the Counselor will not come to you. If I go, I will send him to you. ⁸ When he comes, he will convict the world about sin, righteousness, and judgment: ⁹ About sin, because they do not believe in me; ¹⁰ about righteousness, because I am going to the Father and you will no longer see me; ¹¹ and about judgment, because the ruler of this world has been judged.

¹² "I still have many things to tell you, but you can't bear them now. ¹³ When the Spirit of truth comes, he will guide you into all the truth. For he will not speak on his own, but he will speak whatever he hears. He will also declare to you what is to come. ¹⁴ He will glorify me, because he will take from what is mine and declare it to you. ¹⁵ Everything the Father has is mine. This is why I told you that he takes from what is mine and will declare it to you."

NOTES —————— DAY 17

From Groans

DAY   18

to Glory

ROMANS 8:18–30

From Groans to Glory

[18] For I consider that the sufferings of this present time are not worth comparing with the glory that is going to be revealed to us. [19] For the creation eagerly waits with anticipation for God's sons to be revealed. [20] For the creation was subjected to futility—not willingly, but because of him who subjected it—in the hope [21] that the creation itself will also be set free from the bondage to decay into the glorious freedom of God's children. [22] For we know that the whole creation has been groaning together with labor pains until now. [23] Not only that, but we ourselves who have the Spirit as the firstfruits—

> we also groan within ourselves,
> eagerly waiting for adoption,
> the redemption of our bodies.

[24] Now in this hope we were saved, but hope that is seen is not hope, because who hopes for what he sees? [25] Now if we hope for what we do not see, we eagerly wait for it with patience.

[26] In the same way the Spirit also helps us in our weakness, because we do not know what to pray for as we should, but the Spirit himself intercedes for us with inexpressible groanings. [27] And he who searches our hearts knows the mind of the Spirit, because he intercedes for the saints according to the will of God.

[28] We know that all things work together for the good of those who love God, who are called according to his purpose. [29] For those he foreknew he also predestined to be conformed to the image of his Son, so that he would be the firstborn among many brothers and sisters. [30] And those he predestined, he also called; and those he called, he also justified; and those he justified, he also glorified.

◆ GOING DEEPER

ISAIAH 65:17

"For I will create new heavens and a new earth;
the past events will not be remembered or come to mind."

1 THESSALONIANS 4:13–18

The Comfort of Christ's Coming

[13] We do not want you to be uninformed, brothers and sisters, concerning those who are asleep, so that you will not grieve like the rest, who have no hope. [14] For if we believe that Jesus died and rose again, in the same way, through Jesus, God will bring with him those who have fallen asleep. [15] For we say this to you by a word from the Lord: We who are still alive at the Lord's coming will certainly not precede those who have fallen asleep. [16] For the Lord himself will descend from heaven with a shout, with the archangel's voice, and with the trumpet of God, and the dead in Christ will rise first. [17] Then we who are still alive, who are left, will be caught up together with them in the clouds to meet the Lord in the air, and so we will always be with the Lord. [18] Therefore encourage one another with these words.

REVELATION 21:1–6

The New Creation

[1] Then I saw a new heaven and a new earth; for the first heaven and the first earth had passed away, and the sea was no more. [2] I also saw the holy city, the new Jerusalem, coming down out of heaven from God, prepared like a bride adorned for her husband.

[3] Then I heard a loud voice from the throne: Look, God's dwelling is with humanity, and he will live with them. They will be his peoples, and God himself will be with them and will be their God. [4] He will wipe away every tear from their eyes. Death will be no more; grief, crying, and pain will be no more, because the previous things have passed away.

[5] Then the one seated on the throne said, "Look, I am making everything new." He also said, "Write, because these words are faithful and true." [6] Then he said to me, "It is done! I am the Alpha and the Omega, the beginning and the end. I will freely give to the thirsty from the spring of the water of life."

The Believer's

Triumph

ROMANS 8:31–39

The Believer's Triumph

[31] What, then, are we to say about these things? If God is for us, who is against us? [32] He did not even spare his own Son but gave him up for us all. How will he not also with him grant us everything? [33] Who can bring an accusation against God's elect? God is the one who justifies. [34] Who is the one who condemns? Christ Jesus is the one who died, but even more, has been raised; he also is at the right hand of God and intercedes for us. [35] Who can separate us from the love of Christ? Can affliction or distress or persecution or famine or nakedness or danger or sword? [36] As it is written:

Because of you
we are being put to death all day long;
we are counted as sheep to be slaughtered.

[37] No, in all these things we are more than conquerors through him who loved us.

[38] For I am persuaded that neither death nor life, nor angels nor rulers, nor things present nor things to come, nor powers, [39] nor height nor depth, nor any other created thing will be able to separate us from the love of God that is in Christ Jesus our Lord.

🔖 GOING DEEPER

PSALM 44:17–22

[17] All this has happened to us,
but we have not forgotten you
or betrayed your covenant.
[18] Our hearts have not turned back;
our steps have not strayed from your path.
[19] But you have crushed us in a haunt of jackals
and have covered us with deepest darkness.
[20] If we had forgotten the name of our God
and spread out our hands to a foreign god,
[21] wouldn't God have found this out,
since he knows the secrets of the heart?
[22] Because of you we are being put to death all day long;
we are counted as sheep to be slaughtered.

2 CORINTHIANS 4:7–18

Treasure in Clay Jars

[7] Now we have this treasure in clay jars, so that this extraordinary power may be from God and not from us. [8] We are afflicted in every way but not crushed; we are perplexed but not in despair; [9] we are persecuted but not abandoned; we are struck down but not destroyed. [10] We always carry the death of Jesus in our body, so that the life of Jesus may also be displayed in our body. [11] For we who live are always being given over to death for Jesus's sake, so

that Jesus's life may also be displayed in our mortal flesh. [12] So then, death is at work in us, but life in you. [13] And since we have the same spirit of faith in keeping with what is written, I believed, therefore I spoke, we also believe, and therefore speak. [14] For we know that the one who raised the Lord Jesus will also raise us with Jesus and present us with you. [15] Indeed, everything is for your benefit so that, as grace extends through more and more people, it may cause thanksgiving to increase to the glory of God.

[16] Therefore we do not give up.

Even though our outer person is being destroyed, our inner person is being renewed day by day. [17] For our momentary light affliction is producing for us an absolutely incomparable eternal weight of glory. [18] So we do not focus on what is seen, but on what is unseen. For what is seen is temporary, but what is unseen is eternal.

PHILIPPIANS 1:6

I am sure of this, that he who started a good work in you will carry it on to completion until the day of Christ Jesus.

TAKE ——————— NOTE

Response

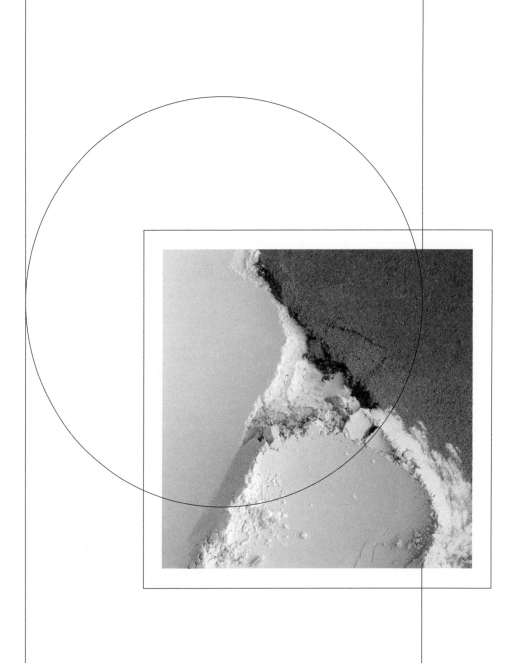

01

Paul's longing for the people of Rome to better understand the truth of the gospel?

02

passages intended to address division or tension?

03

instructions for believers to represent Christ faithfully in their everyday lives?

Take this day to catch up on your reading,
pray, and rest in the presence of the Lord.

I say, then, walk by the Spirit and you will certainly not carry out the desire of the flesh.

GALATIANS 5:16

Weekly

Scripture is God-breathed and true. When we memorize it, we carry the good news of Jesus with us wherever we go.

We are continuing to memorize Romans 3:22–24 by adding verse 23 this week. It is a reminder that every person has sinned and been separated from God.

SEE TIPS FOR MEMORIZING SCRIPTURE ON PAGE (164.)

Truth

ROMANS 3:22–24

²² The righteousness of God is through faith in Jesus Christ to all who believe, since there is no distinction. ²³ For all have sinned and fall short of the glory of God; ²⁴ they are justified freely by his grace through the redemption that is in Christ Jesus.

The God of Mercy

DAY ————————————————— 22

It does not depend on human will or effort but on God who shows mercy.

ROMANS 9:16

ROMANS 9:1–18

Israel's Rejection of Christ

[1] I speak the truth in Christ—I am not lying; my conscience testifies to me through the Holy Spirit— [2] that I have great sorrow and unceasing anguish in my heart. [3] For I could wish that I myself were cursed and cut off from Christ for the benefit of my brothers and sisters, my own flesh and blood. [4] They are Israelites, and to them belong the adoption, the glory, the covenants, the giving of the law, the temple service, and the promises. [5] The ancestors are theirs, and from them, by physical descent, came the Christ, who is God over all, praised forever. Amen.

God's Gracious Election of Israel

[6] Now it is not as though the word of God has failed, because not all who are descended from Israel are Israel. [7] Neither is it the case that all of Abraham's children are his descendants. On the contrary, your offspring will be traced through Isaac. [8] That is, it is not the children by physical descent who are God's children, but the children of the promise are considered to be the offspring. [9] For this is the statement of the promise: At this time I will come, and Sarah will have a son. [10] And not only that, but Rebekah conceived children through one man, our father Isaac. [11] For though her sons had not been born yet or done anything good or bad, so that God's purpose according to election might stand— [12] not from works but from the one who calls—she was told, The older will serve the younger. [13] As it is written: I have loved Jacob, but I have hated Esau.

God's Selection Is Just

[14] What should we say then? Is there injustice with God? Absolutely not! [15] For he tells Moses, I will show mercy to whom I will show mercy, and I will have compassion on whom I will have compassion. [16] So then, it does not depend on human will or effort but on God who shows mercy. [17] For the Scripture tells Pharaoh, I raised you up for this reason so that I may display my power in you and that my name may be proclaimed in the whole earth. [18] So then, he has mercy on whom he wants to have mercy and he hardens whom he wants to harden.

◆ GOING DEEPER

DEUTERONOMY 32:3–12

[3] For I will proclaim the LORD's name.
Declare the greatness of our God!
[4] The Rock—his work is perfect;
all his ways are just.

> A faithful God, without bias,
> he is righteous and true.

[5] His people have acted corruptly toward him;
this is their defect—they are not his children
but a devious and crooked generation.
[6] Is this how you repay the LORD,
you foolish and senseless people?
Isn't he your Father and Creator?
Didn't he make you and sustain you?
[7] Remember the days of old;
consider the years of past generations.
Ask your father, and he will tell you,
your elders, and they will teach you.
[8] When the Most High gave the nations their inheritance
and divided the human race,

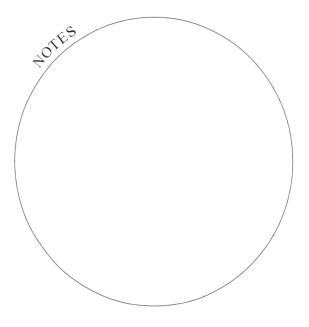

NOTES

he set the boundaries of the peoples
according to the number of the people of Israel.
⁹ But the Lord's portion is his people,
Jacob, his own inheritance.

¹⁰ He found him in a desolate land,
in a barren, howling wilderness;
he surrounded him, cared for him,
and protected him as the pupil of his eye.
¹¹ He watches over his nest like an eagle
and hovers over his young;
he spreads his wings, catches him,
and carries him on his feathers.
¹² The Lord alone led him,
with no help from a foreign god.

EPHESIANS 1:3–6

God's Rich Blessings

³ Blessed is the God and Father of our Lord Jesus Christ, who has blessed us with every spiritual blessing in the heavens in Christ. ⁴ For he chose us in him, before the foundation of the world, to be holy and blameless in love before him. ⁵ He predestined us to be adopted as sons through Jesus Christ for himself, according to the good pleasure of his will,

> ⁶ to the praise of his glorious
> grace that he lavished on us in
> the Beloved One.

NOTES —————— DAY 22

Thus diff'rent powers within me strive,
And death, and sin, by turns, prevail.
I grieve, rejoice, decline, revive,
And vict'ry hangs in doubtful scale:
But Jesus has his promise passed,
That grace shall overcome at last.

—ISABELLA MARSHALL GRAHAM

Objects of Mercy

What if he did this to make known the riches of his glory on objects of mercy...

ROMANS 9:23

ROMANS 9:19–33

¹⁹ You will say to me, therefore, "Why then does he still find fault? For who resists his will?" ²⁰ On the contrary, who are you, a human being, to talk back to God? Will what is formed say to the one who formed it, "Why did you make me like this?" ²¹ Or has the potter no right over the clay, to make from the same lump one piece of pottery for honor and another for dishonor? ²² And what if God, wanting to display his wrath and to make his power known, endured with much patience objects of wrath prepared for destruction? ²³ And what if he did this to make known the riches of his glory on objects of mercy that he prepared beforehand for glory— ²⁴ on us, the ones he also called, not only from the Jews but also from the Gentiles? ²⁵ As it also says in Hosea,

I will call Not My People, My People,
and she who is Unloved, Beloved.
²⁶ And it will be in the place where they were told,
you are not my people,
there they will be called sons of the living God.

²⁷ But Isaiah cries out concerning Israel,

Though the number of Israelites
is like the sand of the sea,
only the remnant will be saved;
²⁸ since the Lord will execute his sentence
completely and decisively on the earth.

²⁹ And just as Isaiah predicted:

If the Lord of Armies had not left us offspring,
we would have become like Sodom,
and we would have been made like Gomorrah.

Israel's Present State

³⁰ What should we say then? Gentiles, who did not pursue righteousness, have obtained righteousness—namely the righteousness that comes from faith. ³¹ But Israel, pursuing the law of righteousness, has not achieved the righteousness of the law. ³² Why is that? Because they did not pursue it by faith, but as if it were by works. They stumbled over the stumbling stone. ³³ As it is written,

Look, I am putting a stone in Zion to stumble over
and a rock to trip over,
and the one who believes on him
will not be put to shame.

♥ GOING DEEPER

JEREMIAH 18:1–6

Parable of the Potter

¹ This is the word that came to Jeremiah from the LORD: ² "Go down at once to the potter's house; there I will reveal my words to you." ³ So I went down to the potter's house, and there he was, working away at the wheel. ⁴ But the jar that he was making from the clay became flawed in the potter's hand, so he made it into another jar, as it seemed right for him to do.

⁵ The word of the LORD came to me: ⁶ "House of Israel, can I not treat you as this potter treats his clay?"—this is the LORD's declaration. "Just like clay in the potter's hand, so are you in my hand, house of Israel."

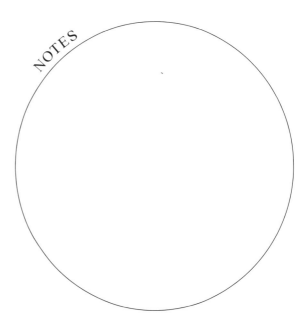

NOTES

EPHESIANS 1:11–14

[11] In him we have also received an inheritance, because we were predestined

> according to the plan of the one who works out
> everything in agreement with the purpose of his will,

[12] so that we who had already put our hope in Christ might bring praise to his glory.

[13] In him you also were sealed with the promised Holy Spirit when you heard the word of truth, the gospel of your salvation, and when you believed. [14] The Holy Spirit is the down payment of our inheritance, until the redemption of the possession, to the praise of his glory.

NOTES ————— DAY 23

Righteousness

by Faith Alone

ROMANS 10

Righteousness by Faith Alone

¹ Brothers and sisters, my heart's desire and prayer to God concerning them is for their salvation. ² I can testify about them that they have zeal for God, but not according to knowledge. ³ Since they are ignorant of the righteousness of God and attempted to establish their own righteousness, they have not submitted to God's righteousness. ⁴ For Christ is the end of the law for righteousness to everyone who believes, ⁵ since Moses writes about the righteousness that is from the law: The one who does these things will live by them. ⁶ But the righteousness that comes from faith speaks like this: Do not say in your heart, "Who will go up to heaven?" that is, to bring Christ down ⁷ or, "Who will go down into the abyss?" that is, to bring Christ up from the dead. ⁸ On the contrary, what does it say? The message is near you, in your mouth and in your heart. This is the message of faith that we proclaim:

> ⁹ If you confess with your mouth, "Jesus is Lord," and believe in your heart that God raised him from the dead, you will be saved.

¹⁰ One believes with the heart, resulting in righteousness, and one confesses with the mouth, resulting in salvation. ¹¹ For the Scripture says, Everyone who believes on him will not be put to shame, ¹² since there is no distinction between Jew and Greek, because the same Lord of all richly blesses all who call on him. ¹³ For everyone who calls on the name of the Lord will be saved.

Israel's Rejection of the Message

¹⁴ How, then, can they call on him they have not believed in? And how can they believe without hearing about him? And how can they hear without a preacher? ¹⁵ And how can they preach unless they are sent? As it is written: How beautiful are the feet of those who bring good news. ¹⁶ But not all obeyed the gospel. For Isaiah says, Lord, who has believed our message? ¹⁷ So faith comes from what is heard, and what is heard comes through the message about Christ. ¹⁸ But I ask, "Did they not hear?" Yes, they did:

Their voice has gone out to the whole earth,
and their words to the ends of the world.

¹⁹ But I ask, "Did Israel not understand?" First, Moses said,

I will make you jealous
of those who are not a nation;
I will make you angry by a nation
that lacks understanding.

²⁰ And Isaiah says boldly,

I was found
by those who were not looking for me;
I revealed myself
to those who were not asking for me.

²¹ But to Israel he says, All day long I have held out my hands to a disobedient and defiant people.

NOTES

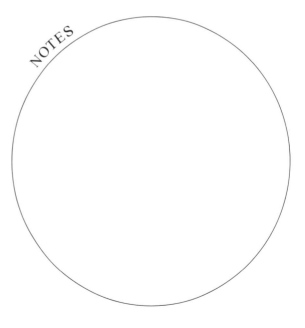

JOEL 2:32

Then everyone who calls
on the name of the Lord will be saved,
for there will be an escape
for those on Mount Zion and in Jerusalem,
as the Lord promised,
among the survivors the Lord calls.

GALATIANS 3:7–14

[7] You know, then, that those who have faith, these are Abraham's sons.

[8] Now the Scripture saw in advance that God would justify the Gentiles by faith and proclaimed the gospel ahead of time to Abraham, saying, All the nations will be blessed through you. [9] Consequently, those who have faith are blessed with Abraham, who had faith.

Law and Promise

[10] For all who rely on the works of the law are under a curse, because it is written, Everyone who does not do everything written in the book of the law is cursed. [11] Now it is clear that no one is justified before God by the law, because the righteous will live by faith. [12] But the law is not based on faith; instead, the one who does these things will live by them. [13] Christ redeemed us from the curse of the law by becoming a curse for us, because it is written, Cursed is everyone who is hung on a tree. [14] The purpose was that the blessing of Abraham would come to the Gentiles by Christ Jesus, so that we could receive the promised Spirit through faith.

NOTES ——————— DAY 24

Paul's Responses to Key Issues

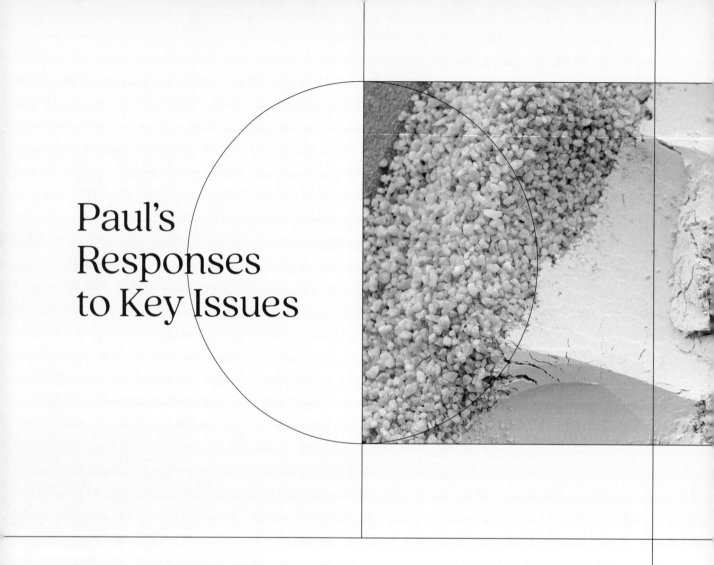

The early Church was made up of Jewish and Gentile believers with cultural, religious, and traditional differences. Tensions frequently arose among these new, diverse groups of believers as they learned how to live out the gospel together in community. Keeping the true gospel as the standard, Paul addressed these issues or "disputable matters," measuring each to determine whether they were essential or nonessential components of the faith. This helped determine if the issue should prompt someone to remain united in the gospel or to break fellowship because of opposition to the reality of the gospel.

Included here are some of the key issues addressed in the book of Romans that arose among believers in the first century, along with whether or not those issues were grounds for believers to break fellowship.

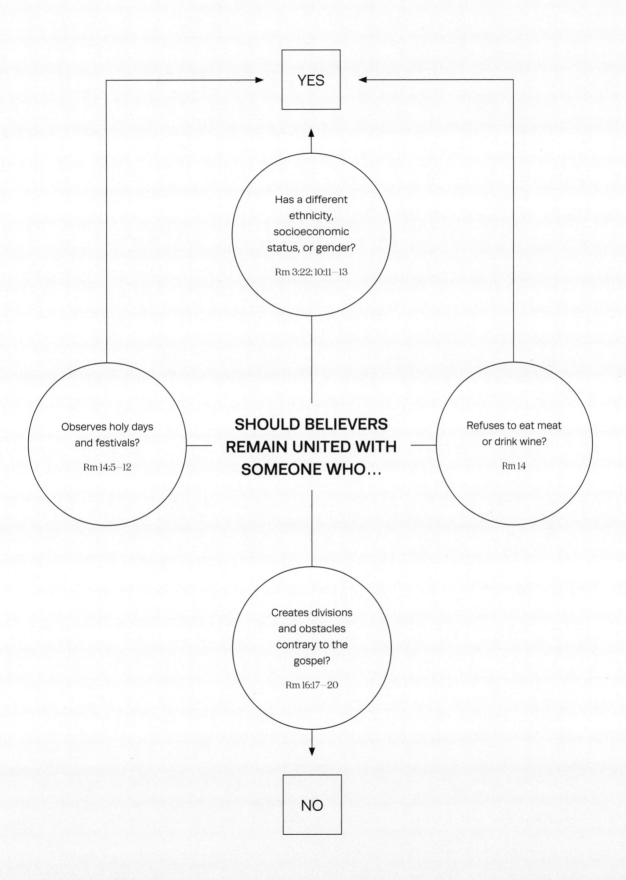

YES

Has a different
ethnicity,
socioeconomic
status, or gender?

Rm 3:22; 10:11—13

Observes holy days
and festivals?

Rm 14:5—12

SHOULD BELIEVERS
REMAIN UNITED WITH
SOMEONE WHO…

Refuses to eat meat
or drink wine?

Rm 14

Creates divisions
and obstacles
contrary to the
gospel?

Rm 16:17—20

NO

God Has Not

Rejected His People

ROMANS 11

Israel's Rejection Not Total

¹ I ask, then, has God rejected his people? Absolutely not! For I too am an Israelite, a descendant of Abraham, from the tribe of Benjamin. ² God has not rejected his people whom he foreknew. Or don't you know what the Scripture says in the passage about Elijah—how he pleads with God against Israel? ³ Lord, they have killed your prophets and torn down your altars. I am the only one left, and they are trying to take my life! ⁴ But what was God's answer to him? I have left seven thousand for myself who have not bowed down to Baal. ⁵ In the same way, then, there is also at the present time

a remnant chosen by grace.

⁶ Now if by grace, then it is not by works; otherwise grace ceases to be grace.

⁷ What then? Israel did not find what it was looking for, but the elect did find it. The rest were hardened, ⁸ as it is written,

> God gave them a spirit of stupor,
> eyes that cannot see
> and ears that cannot hear,
> to this day.

⁹ And David says,

> Let their table become a snare and a trap,
> a pitfall and a retribution to them.

> ¹⁰ Let their eyes be darkened so that they cannot see,
> and their backs be bent continually.

Israel's Rejection Not Final

¹¹ I ask, then, have they stumbled so as to fall? Absolutely not! On the contrary, by their transgression, salvation has come to the Gentiles to make Israel jealous. ¹² Now if their transgression brings riches for the world, and their failure riches for the Gentiles, how much more will their fullness bring!

¹³ Now I am speaking to you Gentiles. Insofar as I am an apostle to the Gentiles, I magnify my ministry, ¹⁴ if I might somehow make my own people jealous and save some of them. ¹⁵ For if their rejection brings reconciliation to the world, what will their acceptance mean but life from the dead? ¹⁶ Now if the firstfruits are holy, so is the whole batch. And if the root is holy, so are the branches.

¹⁷ Now if some of the branches were broken off, and you, though a wild olive branch, were grafted in among them and have come to share in the rich root of the cultivated olive tree, ¹⁸ do not boast that you are better than those branches. But if you do boast—you do not sustain the root, but the root sustains you. ¹⁹ Then you will say, "Branches were broken off so that I might be grafted in." ²⁰ True enough; they were broken off because of unbelief, but you stand by

faith. Do not be arrogant, but beware, [21] because if God did not spare the natural branches, he will not spare you either. [22] Therefore, consider God's kindness and severity: severity toward those who have fallen but God's kindness toward you—if you remain in his kindness. Otherwise you too will be cut off. [23] And even they, if they do not remain in unbelief, will be grafted in, because God has the power to graft them in again. [24] For if you were cut off from your native wild olive tree and against nature were grafted into a cultivated olive tree, how much more will these—the natural branches—be grafted into their own olive tree?

[25] I don't want you to be ignorant of this mystery, brothers and sisters, so that you will not be conceited: A partial hardening has come upon Israel until the fullness of the Gentiles has come in. [26] And in this way all Israel will be saved, as it is written,

> The Deliverer will come from Zion;
> he will turn godlessness away from Jacob.
> [27] And this will be my covenant with them
> when I take away their sins.

[28] Regarding the gospel, they are enemies for your advantage, but regarding election, they are loved because of the patriarchs, [29] since God's gracious gifts and calling are irrevocable. [30] As you once disobeyed God but now have received mercy through their disobedience, [31] so they too have now disobeyed, resulting in mercy to you, so that they also may now receive mercy. [32] For God has imprisoned all in disobedience so that he may have mercy on all.

A Hymn of Praise

> [33] Oh, the depth of the riches
> and the wisdom and the knowledge of God!
> How unsearchable his judgments
> and untraceable his ways!
> [34] For who has known the mind of the Lord?
> Or who has been his counselor?
> [35] And who has ever given to God,
> that he should be repaid?
> [36] For from him and through him
> and to him are all things.
> To him be the glory forever. Amen.

HOSEA 14:4–7

A Promise of Restoration

[4] "I will heal their apostasy;
I will freely love them,
for my anger will have turned from him.
[5] I will be like the dew to Israel;
he will blossom like the lily
and take root like the cedars of Lebanon.
[6] His new branches will spread,
and his splendor will be like the olive tree,
his fragrance, like the forest of Lebanon.

[7] The people will return and live beneath his shade.

They will grow grain
and blossom like the vine.
His renown will be like the wine of Lebanon."

1 PETER 2:7–10

[7] So honor will come to you who believe; but for the unbelieving,

The stone that the builders rejected—
this one has become the cornerstone,

[8] and

A stone to stumble over,
and a rock to trip over.

They stumble because they disobey the word; they were destined for this.

[9] But you are a chosen race, a royal priesthood, a holy nation, a people for his possession, so that you may proclaim the praises of the one who called you out of darkness into his marvelous light. [10] Once you were not a people, but now you are God's people; you had not received mercy, but now you have received mercy.

NOTES ———— DAY 25

Many Gifts

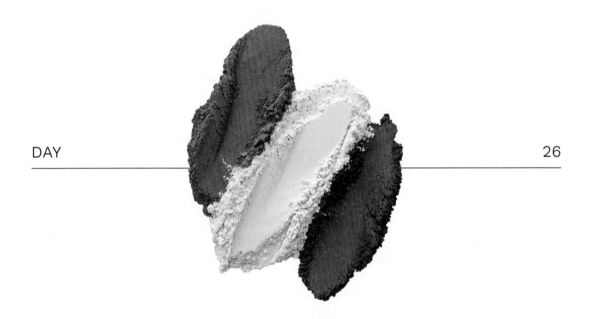

but One Body

ROMANS 12:1–8

A Living Sacrifice

¹ Therefore, brothers and sisters, in view of the mercies of God, I urge you to present your bodies as a living sacrifice, holy and pleasing to God; this is your true worship. ² Do not be conformed to this age, but be transformed by the renewing of your mind, so that you may discern what is the good, pleasing, and perfect will of God.

Many Gifts but One Body

³ For by the grace given to me, I tell everyone among you not to think of himself more highly than he should think. Instead, think sensibly, as God has distributed a measure of faith to each one. ⁴ Now as we have many parts in one body, and all the parts do not have the same function, ⁵ in the same way we who are many are one body in Christ and individually members of one another.

> ⁶ According to the grace given to us, we have different gifts:

If prophecy, use it according to the proportion of one's faith; ⁷ if service, use it in service; if teaching, in teaching; ⁸ if exhorting, in exhortation; giving, with generosity; leading, with diligence; showing mercy, with cheerfulness.

◆ GOING DEEPER

1 CORINTHIANS 12:12–14

Unity Yet Diversity in the Body

¹² For just as the body is one and has many parts, and all the parts of that body, though many, are one body—so also is Christ. ¹³ For we were all baptized by one Spirit into one body—whether Jews or Greeks, whether slaves or free—and we were all given one Spirit to drink. ¹⁴ Indeed, the body is not one part but many.

EPHESIANS 4:1–16

Unity and Diversity in the Body of Christ

¹ Therefore I, the prisoner in the Lord, urge you to walk worthy of the calling you have received, ² with all humility

and gentleness, with patience, bearing with one another in love, ³ making every effort to keep the unity of the Spirit through the bond of peace.

> ⁴ There is one body and one Spirit—just as you were called to one hope at your calling— ⁵ one Lord, one faith, one baptism, ⁶ one God and Father of all, who is above all and through all and in all.

⁷ Now grace was given to each one of us according to the measure of Christ's gift. ⁸ For it says:

> When he ascended on high,
> he took the captives captive;
> he gave gifts to people.

⁹ But what does "he ascended" mean except that he also descended to the lower parts of the earth? ¹⁰ The one who descended is also the one who ascended far above all the heavens, to fill all things. ¹¹ And he himself gave some to be apostles, some prophets, some evangelists, some pastors and teachers, ¹² to equip the saints for the work of ministry, to build up the body of Christ, ¹³ until we all reach unity in the faith and in the knowledge of God's Son, growing into maturity with a stature measured by Christ's fullness. ¹⁴ Then we will no longer be little children, tossed by the waves and blown around by every wind of teaching, by human cunning with cleverness in the techniques of deceit. ¹⁵ But speaking the truth in love, let us grow in every way into him who is the head—Christ. ¹⁶ From him the whole body, fitted and knit together by every supporting ligament, promotes the growth of the body for building itself up in love by the proper working of each individual part.

NOTES ———— DAY 26

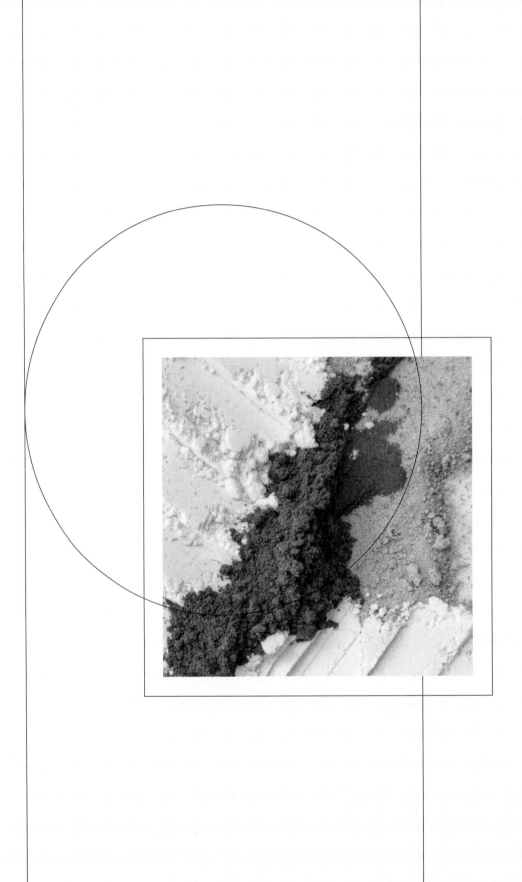

Response

IN THIS WEEK'S READING, WHERE DID I SEE...

01

Paul's longing for the people of Rome to better understand the truth of the gospel?

02

passages intended to address division or tension?

03

instructions for believers to represent Christ faithfully in their everyday lives?

Take this day to catch up on your reading,
pray, and rest in the presence of the Lord.

Now it is clear that no one is justified before God by the law, because the righteous will live by faith.

GALATIANS 3:11

Weekly

Scripture is God-breathed and true. When we memorize it, we carry the good news of Jesus with us wherever we go.

This week we'll add our final verse as we memorize Romans 3:22–24, remembering that it is only by God's grace that we can experience the redemption of Jesus.

SEE TIPS FOR MEMORIZING SCRIPTURE ON PAGE (164.)

Truth

ROMANS 3:22–24

²² The righteousness of God is through faith in Jesus Christ to all who believe, since there is no distinction. ²³ For all have sinned and fall short of the glory of God; ²⁴ they are justified freely by his grace through the redemption that is in Christ Jesus.

Christian

DAY
29

Ethics

ROMANS 12:9–21

Christian Ethics

[9] Let love be without hypocrisy. Detest evil; cling to what is good. [10] Love one another deeply as brothers and sisters. Take the lead in honoring one another. [11] Do not lack diligence in zeal; be fervent in the Spirit; serve the Lord. [12] Rejoice in hope; be patient in affliction; be persistent in prayer. [13] Share with the saints in their needs; pursue hospitality. [14] Bless those who persecute you; bless and do not curse. [15] Rejoice with those who rejoice; weep with those who weep. [16] Live in harmony with one another. Do not be proud; instead, associate with the humble. Do not be wise in your own estimation. [17] Do not repay anyone evil for evil. Give careful thought to do what is honorable in everyone's eyes.

> [18] If possible, as far as it depends on you, live at peace with everyone.

[19] Friends, do not avenge yourselves; instead, leave room for God's wrath, because it is written, Vengeance belongs to me; I will repay, says the Lord. [20] But

> If your enemy is hungry, feed him.
> If he is thirsty, give him something to drink.
> For in so doing
> you will be heaping fiery coals on his head.

[21] Do not be conquered by evil, but conquer evil with good.

◆ GOING DEEPER

AMOS 5:14–15

[14] Pursue good and not evil
so that you may live,
and the Lord, the God of Armies,
will be with you
as you have claimed.
[15] Hate evil and love good;
establish justice at the city gate.
Perhaps the Lord, the God of Armies, will be gracious
to the remnant of Joseph.

MATTHEW 22:34–39

The Primary Commands

[34] When the Pharisees heard that he had silenced the Sadducees, they came together. [35] And one of them, an expert in the law, asked a question to test him: [36] "Teacher, which command in the law is the greatest?"

[37] He said to him, "Love the Lord your God with all your heart, with all your soul, and with all your mind. [38] This is the greatest and most important command. [39] The second is like it: Love your neighbor as yourself."

NOTES ——————— DAY 29

Love, Our Primary Duty

DAY ———————————————— 30

...for the one who loves
another has fulfilled the law.

ROMANS 13:8

ROMANS 13

A Christian's Duties to the State

[1] Let everyone submit to the governing authorities, since there is no authority except from God, and the authorities that exist are instituted by God. [2] So then, the one who resists the authority is opposing God's command, and those who oppose it will bring judgment on themselves. [3] For rulers are not a terror to good conduct, but to bad. Do you want to be unafraid of the one in authority? Do what is good, and you will have its approval. [4] For it is God's servant for your good. But if you do wrong, be afraid, because it does not carry the sword for no reason. For it is God's servant, an avenger that brings wrath on the one who does wrong. [5] Therefore, you must submit, not only because of wrath but also because of your conscience. [6] And for this reason you pay taxes, since the authorities are God's servants, continually attending to these tasks. [7] Pay your obligations to everyone: taxes to those you owe taxes, tolls to those you owe tolls, respect to those you owe respect, and honor to those you owe honor.

Love, Our Primary Duty

[8] Do not owe anyone anything, except to love one another, for the one who loves another has fulfilled the law. [9] The commandments, Do not commit adultery; do not murder; do not steal; do not covet; and any other commandment, are summed up by this commandment:

Love your neighbor as yourself.

[10] Love does no wrong to a neighbor. Love, therefore, is the fulfillment of the law.

Put On Christ

[11] Besides this, since you know the time, it is already the hour for you to wake up from sleep, because now our salvation is nearer than when we first believed. [12] The night is nearly over, and the day is near; so let us discard the deeds of darkness and put on the armor of light. [13] Let us walk with decency, as in the daytime: not in carousing and drunkenness; not in sexual impurity and promiscuity; not in quarreling and jealousy. [14] But put on the Lord Jesus Christ, and make no provision for the flesh to gratify its desires.

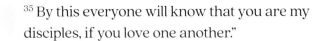 GOING DEEPER

JOHN 13:34–35

³⁴ "I give you a new command: Love one another. Just as I have loved you, you are also to love one another.

³⁵ By this everyone will know that you are my disciples, if you love one another."

HEBREWS 13:15–17

¹⁵ Therefore, through him let us continually offer up to God a sacrifice of praise, that is, the fruit of lips that confess his name. ¹⁶ Don't neglect to do what is good and to share, for God is pleased with such sacrifices. ¹⁷ Obey your leaders and submit to them, since they keep watch over your souls as those who will give an account, so that they can do this with joy and not with grief, for that would be unprofitable for you.

NOTES —————— DAY 30

The Law

of Love

ROMANS 14

The Law of Liberty

[1] Welcome anyone who is weak in faith, but don't argue about disputed matters. [2] One person believes he may eat anything, while one who is weak eats only vegetables. [3] One who eats must not look down on one who does not eat, and one who does not eat must not judge one who does, because God has accepted him. [4] Who are you to judge another's household servant? Before his own Lord he stands or falls. And he will stand, because the Lord is able to make him stand.

[5] One person judges one day to be more important than another day. Someone else judges every day to be the same. Let each one be fully convinced in his own mind. [6] Whoever observes the day, observes it for the honor of the Lord. Whoever eats, eats for the Lord, since he gives thanks to God; and whoever does not eat, it is for the Lord that he does not eat it, and he gives thanks to God. [7] For none of us lives for himself, and no one dies for himself. [8] If we live, we live for the Lord; and if we die, we die for the Lord. Therefore, whether we live or die, we belong to the Lord. [9] Christ died and returned to life for this: that he might be Lord over both the dead and the living. [10] But you, why do you judge your brother or sister? Or you, why do you despise your brother or sister? For we will all stand before the judgment seat of God. [11] For it is written,

As I live, says the Lord,
every knee will bow to me,
and every tongue will give praise to God.

[12] So then, each of us will give an account of himself to God.

The Law of Love

[13] Therefore, let us no longer judge one another. Instead decide never to put a stumbling block or pitfall in the way of your brother or sister. [14] I know and am persuaded in the Lord Jesus that nothing is unclean in itself. Still, to someone who considers a thing to be unclean, to that one it is unclean. [15] For if your brother or sister is hurt by what you eat, you are no longer walking according to love. Do not destroy, by what you eat, someone for whom Christ died. [16] Therefore, do not let your good be slandered, [17] for the kingdom of God is not eating and drinking, but righteousness, peace, and joy in the Holy Spirit. [18] Whoever serves Christ in this way is acceptable to God and receives human approval.

[19] So then, let us pursue what promotes peace and what builds up one another. [20] Do not tear down God's work because of food. Everything is clean, but it is wrong to make someone fall by what he eats. [21] It is a good thing not to eat meat, or drink wine, or do anything that makes your brother

or sister stumble. ²² Whatever you believe about these things, keep between yourself and God. Blessed is the one who does not condemn himself by what he approves. ²³ But whoever doubts stands condemned if he eats, because his eating is not from faith, and everything that is not from faith is sin.

◗ GOING DEEPER

1 CORINTHIANS 8:8–13

⁸ Food will not bring us close to God. We are not worse off if we don't eat, and we are not better if we do eat.

> ⁹ But be careful that this right of yours in no way becomes a stumbling block to the weak.

¹⁰ For if someone sees you, the one who has knowledge, dining in an idol's temple, won't his weak conscience be encouraged to eat food offered to idols? ¹¹ So the weak person, the brother or sister for whom Christ died, is ruined by your knowledge. ¹² Now when you sin like this against brothers and sisters and wound their weak conscience, you are sinning against Christ. ¹³ Therefore, if food causes my brother or sister to fall, I will never again eat meat, so that I won't cause my brother or sister to fall.

COLOSSIANS 2:16–17

¹⁶ Therefore, don't let anyone judge you in regard to food and drink or in the matter of a festival or a new moon or a Sabbath day. ¹⁷ These are a shadow of what was to come; the substance is Christ.

TAKE ——— NOTE

Glorifying God Together

Therefore welcome one another, just as Christ also welcomed you.

ROMANS 15:7

ROMANS 15

Pleasing Others, Not Ourselves

¹ Now we who are strong have an obligation to bear the weaknesses of those without strength, and not to please ourselves. ² Each one of us is to please his neighbor for his good, to build him up. ³ For even Christ did not please himself. On the contrary, as it is written, The insults of those who insult you have fallen on me. ⁴ For whatever was written in the past was written for our instruction, so that we may have hope through endurance and through the encouragement from the Scriptures. ⁵ Now may the God who gives endurance and encouragement grant you to live in harmony with one another, according to Christ Jesus, ⁶ so that you may glorify the God and Father of our Lord Jesus Christ with one mind and one voice.

Glorifying God Together

⁷ Therefore welcome one another, just as Christ also welcomed you, to the glory of God. ⁸ For I say that Christ became a servant of the circumcised on behalf of God's truth, to confirm the promises to the fathers, ⁹ and

> ## so that Gentiles may glorify God for his mercy.

As it is written,

> Therefore I will praise you among the Gentiles,
> and I will sing praise to your name.

¹⁰ Again it says, Rejoice, you Gentiles, with his people! ¹¹ And again,

> Praise the Lord, all you Gentiles;
> let all the peoples praise him!

¹² And again, Isaiah says,

> The root of Jesse will appear,
> the one who rises to rule the Gentiles;
> the Gentiles will hope in him.

¹³ Now may the God of hope fill you with all joy and peace as you believe so that you may overflow with hope by the power of the Holy Spirit.

From Jerusalem to Illyricum

¹⁴ My brothers and sisters, I myself am convinced about you that you also are full of goodness, filled with all knowledge, and able to instruct one another. ¹⁵ Nevertheless, I have written to remind you more boldly on some points because of the grace given me by God ¹⁶ to be a minister of Christ Jesus to the Gentiles, serving as a priest of the gospel of God. God's purpose is that the Gentiles may be an acceptable offering, sanctified by the Holy Spirit. ¹⁷ Therefore I have reason to boast in Christ Jesus regarding what pertains to God. ¹⁸ For I would not dare say anything except what Christ has accomplished through me by word and deed for the obedience of the Gentiles, ¹⁹ by the power of miraculous signs and wonders, and by the power of God's Spirit. As a result, I have fully proclaimed the gospel of Christ from

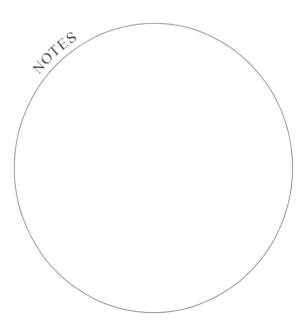

NOTES

Jerusalem all the way around to <u>Illyricum</u>. [20] My aim is to preach the gospel where Christ has not been named, so that I will not build on someone else's foundation, [21] but, as it is written,

> Those who were not told about him will see,
> and those who have not heard will understand.

Paul's Travel Plans

[22] That is why I have been prevented many times from coming to you. [23] But now I no longer have any work to do in these regions, and I have strongly desired for many years to come to you [24] whenever I travel to <u>Spain</u>. For I hope to see you when I pass through and to be assisted by you for my journey there, once I have first enjoyed your company for a while. [25] Right now I am traveling to Jerusalem to serve the saints, [26] because Macedonia and Achaia were pleased to make a contribution for the poor among the saints in Jerusalem. [27] Yes, they were pleased, and indeed are indebted to them. For if the Gentiles have shared in their spiritual benefits, then they are obligated to minister to them in material needs. [28] So when I have finished this and safely delivered the funds to them, I will visit you on the way to Spain. [29] I know that when I come to you, I will come in the fullness of the blessing of Christ.

[30] Now I appeal to you, brothers and sisters, through our Lord Jesus Christ and through the love of the Spirit, to strive together with me in prayers to God on my behalf. [31] Pray that I may be rescued from the unbelievers in Judea, that my ministry to Jerusalem may be acceptable to the saints, [32] and that, by God's will, I may come to you with joy and be refreshed together with you.

[33] May the God of peace be with all of you. Amen.

♥ GOING DEEPER

2 SAMUEL 22:50–51

[50] Therefore I will give thanks to you among the nations, LORD;
I will sing praises about your name.
[51] He is a tower of salvation for his king;
he shows loyalty to his anointed,
to David and his descendants forever.

PSALM 117

Universal Call to Praise
[1] Praise the LORD, all nations!
Glorify him, all peoples!
[2] For his faithful love to us is great;
the LORD's faithfulness endures forever.
Hallelujah!

Illyricum was the furthest point Paul had proclaimed the gospel when he wrote this letter.

Spain was hundreds of miles beyond any place Paul had traveled to before.

NOTES ——————— DAY 32

The Christian Church in Rome

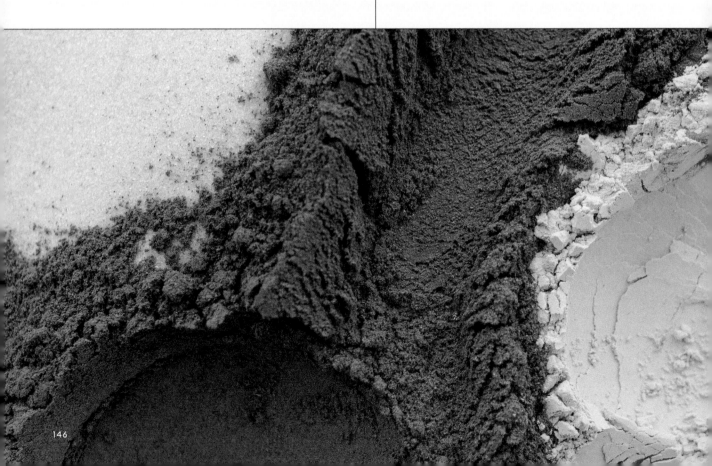

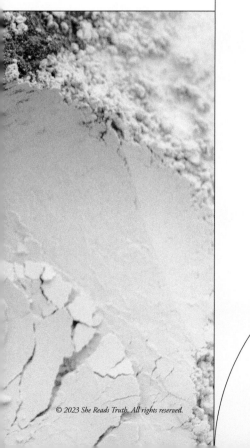

The Christians in Rome reflected the diversity of the Roman Empire itself. The believers, from different religious backgrounds, regions, and socioeconomic statuses, experienced tension and division over a number of issues. In writing to the Roman church, Paul called this group to find unity in their faith.

Paul was not the person who brought the gospel to Rome, nor had he visited these believers before sending this letter (Rm 1:10, 13). Yet this letter ends with a lengthy list of people the recipients are to greet. To greet someone was an expression of fellowship, an act of recognizing others as engaged in the same kingdom work of serving the Lord.

On the following pages is a look at what the book of Romans tells us about the diverse groups of people present in Rome that Paul called to be reconciled in the gospel.

House Churches

Jewish Believers

Christians in Paul's time met together in smaller groups, gathering in the homes of wealthier believers or in places of business. The last chapter of Romans suggests there were at least five gatherings, or house churches, in Rome.

Household of Prisca (also known as Priscilla) and Aquila
Rm 16:3—5

Household of Aristobulus
Rm 16:10—11

Household of Narcissus
Rm 16:10—11

Household of Asyncritus, Phlegon, Hermas, Patrobas, and Hermes
Rm 16:14—15

Household of Philologus, Julia, Nereus, and Olympas
Rm 16:14—15

The earliest Christians in Rome were likely Jewish Romans who came to faith at Pentecost while in Jerusalem (Ac 2:10). However, in AD 49 the emperor Claudius expelled all Jewish people from Rome, including Jewish converts to Christianity (Ac 18:2). Once the Jewish people were permitted to return a few years later, Jewish believers made their way back to Rome.

Gentile Believers

When all Jewish people were expelled from Rome, the local population of non-Jewish (Gentile) believers and leadership grew. This group reflected the diversity of Rome itself. Of the people mentioned by name in Romans, there is a possible immigrant to Rome from Asia (Epaenetus), those with Latin names (e.g., Urbanus and Julia), Greek names (e.g., Stachys, Aristobulus, and Philologus), and an eastern name (Persis).

The Weak and Strong

Paul describes those who are "weak" as being at odds with those described as "strong." Though scholars disagree about who would be categorized in each group, it seems that the differences pertained to food laws, the celebration of Jewish festivals, circumcision, and other issues around how much Christians should adhere to the law of Moses. Similar to Paul's use of these terms to the Corinthian church (1Co 8:7–13), the "weak" likely referred to those who believed it was necessary to continue obeying the law. The "strong" would then be those who believed obedience to the law was not essential.

Marginalized in Society

Many of the members of the church in Rome were likely those who were more marginalized in society based on gender, social hierarchy, or socioeconomic status. Several of the people listed, like Ampliatus, Hermes, and Patrobas, are believed to have been enslaved people or formerly enslaved people. Nine women are also greeted in chapter 16, either by name or description. The list includes Prisca (Priscilla), Junia, Tryphaena, and Tryphosa.

Now to him who is able to strengthen you according to my gospel... ROMANS 16:25

To Him Who Is Able

ROMANS 16

Paul's Commendation of Phoebe

[1] I commend to you our sister Phoebe, who is a servant of the church in Cenchreae. [2] So you should welcome her in the Lord in a manner worthy of the saints and assist her in whatever matter she may require your help. For indeed she has been a benefactor of many—and of me also.

Greeting to Roman Christians

[3] Give my greetings to Prisca and Aquila, my coworkers in Christ Jesus, [4] who risked their own necks for my life. Not only do I thank them, but so do all the Gentile churches. [5] Greet also the church that meets in their home. Greet my dear friend Epaenetus, who is the first convert to Christ from Asia. [6] Greet Mary, who has worked very hard for you. [7] Greet Andronicus and Junia, my fellow Jews and fellow prisoners. They are noteworthy in the eyes of the apostles, and they were also in Christ before me. [8] Greet Ampliatus, my dear friend in the Lord. [9] Greet Urbanus, our coworker in Christ, and my dear friend Stachys. [10] Greet Apelles, who is approved in Christ. Greet those who belong to the household of Aristobulus. [11] Greet Herodion, my fellow Jew. Greet those who belong to the household of Narcissus who are in the Lord. [12] Greet Tryphaena and Tryphosa, who have worked hard in the Lord. Greet my dear friend Persis, who has worked very hard in the Lord. [13] Greet Rufus, chosen in the Lord; also his mother—and mine. [14] Greet Asyncritus, Phlegon, Hermes, Patrobas, Hermas, and the brothers and sisters who are with them. [15] Greet Philologus and Julia, Nereus and his sister, and Olympas, and all the saints who are with them. [16] Greet one another with a holy kiss. All the churches of Christ send you greetings.

Warning Against Divisive People

[17] Now I urge you, brothers and sisters, to watch out for those who create divisions and obstacles contrary to the teaching that you learned. Avoid them, [18] because such people do not serve our Lord Christ but their own appetites. They deceive the hearts of the unsuspecting with smooth talk and flattering words.

Paul's Gracious Conclusion

[19] The report of your obedience has reached everyone. Therefore I rejoice over you, but I want you to be wise about what is good, and yet innocent about what is evil. [20] The God of peace will soon crush Satan under your feet. The grace of our Lord Jesus be with you.

[21] Timothy, my coworker, and Lucius, Jason, and Sosipater, my fellow countrymen, greet you.

[22] I, Tertius, who wrote this letter, greet you in the Lord.

Phoebe carried Paul's letter from Corinth to the church at Rome, a journey spanning hundreds of miles and requiring travel by both land and sea.

Paul first met Prisca (Priscilla) and Aquila when he was in Corinth on his second missionary journey. This visit was about seven years before he visited Corinth again on his third missionary journey, when he wrote this letter to the Romans.

Paul first met Timothy in the city of Lystra on his second missionary journey.

[23] Gaius, who is host to me and to the whole church, greets you. Erastus, the city treasurer, and our brother Quartus greet you.

Glory to God

[25] Now to him who is able to strengthen you according to my gospel and the proclamation about Jesus Christ, according to the revelation of the mystery kept silent for long ages [26] but now revealed and made known through the prophetic Scriptures, according to the command of the eternal God to advance the obedience of faith among all the Gentiles— [27] to the only wise God, through Jesus Christ—to him be the glory forever! Amen.

♥ GOING DEEPER

EPHESIANS 3:20–21

[20] Now to him who is able to do above and beyond all that we ask or think according to the power that works in us— [21] to him be glory in the church and in Christ Jesus to all generations, forever and ever. Amen.

JUDE 24–25

[24] Now to him who is able to protect you from stumbling and to make you stand in the presence of his glory, without blemish and with great joy,

> [25] to the only God our Savior, through Jesus Christ our Lord, be glory, majesty, power, and authority before all time, now and forever. Amen.

Response

01

Paul's longing for the people of Rome to better understand the truth of the gospel?

02

passages intended to address division or tension?

03

instructions for believers to represent Christ faithfully in their everyday lives?

Take this day to catch up on your reading,
pray, and rest in the presence of the Lord.

"I give you a new
command: Love one
another. Just as I have
loved you, you are also
to love one another."

JOHN 13:34

Weekly

DAY ———————————————————

Scripture is God-breathed and true. When we memorize it, we carry the good news of Jesus with us wherever we go.

For this final week, review Romans 3:22–24 in its entirety as you commit it to memory. Remember this gospel reality that redemption and righteousness are available to all who trust in Christ Jesus.

SEE TIPS FOR MEMORIZING SCRIPTURE ON PAGE 164.

Truth

ROMANS 3:22–24

²² <u>The righteousness of God is through faith in Jesus Christ to all who believe, since there is no distinction.</u> ²³ <u>For all have sinned and fall short of the glory of God;</u> ²⁴ <u>they are justified freely by his grace through the redemption that is in Christ Jesus.</u>

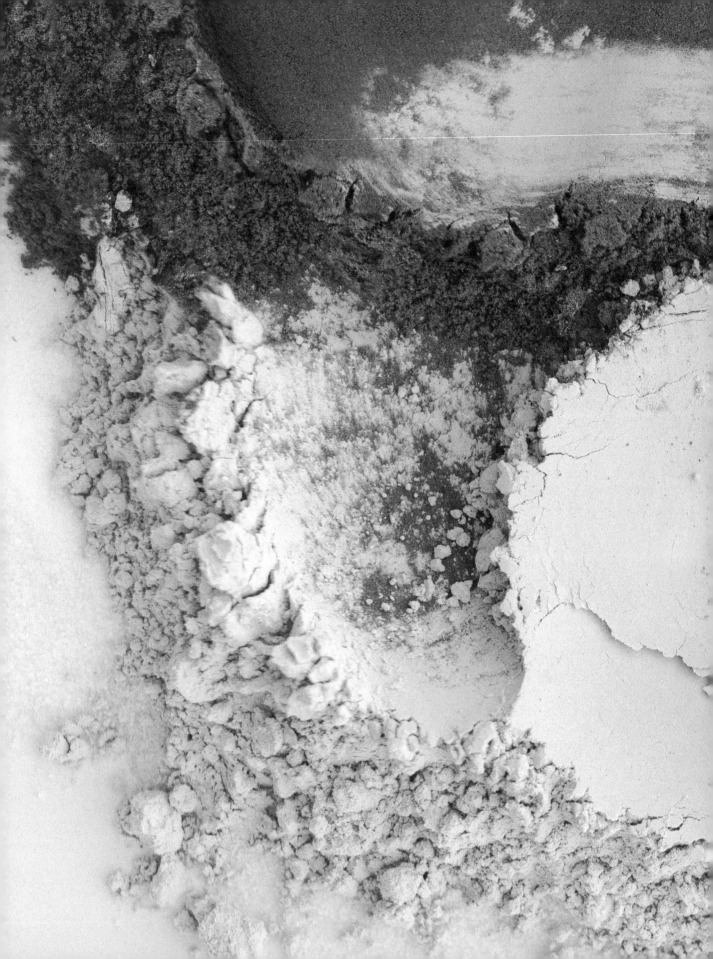

Now may the God of hope
fill you with all joy and peace
as you believe so that you
may overflow with hope by
the power of the Holy Spirit.

ROMANS 15:13

Tips for Memorizing Scripture

At She Reads Truth, we believe Scripture memorization is an important discipline in your walk with God. Committing God's Truth to memory means He can minister to us—and we can minister to others—through His Word no matter where we are. As you approach the Weekly Truth passage in this book, try these memorization tips to see which techniques work best for you!

STUDY IT

Study the passage in its biblical context and ask yourself a few questions before you begin to memorize it: What does this passage say? What does it mean? How would I say this in my own words? What does it teach me about God? Understanding what the passage means helps you know why it is important to carry it with you wherever you go.

Break the passage into smaller sections, memorizing a phrase at a time.

PRAY IT

Use the passage you are memorizing as a prompt for prayer.

WRITE IT

Dedicate a notebook to Scripture memorization and write the passage over and over again.

Diagram the passage after you write it out. Place a square around the verbs, underline the nouns, and circle any adjectives or adverbs. Say the passage aloud several times, emphasizing the verbs as you repeat it. Then do the same thing again with the nouns, then the adjectives and adverbs.

Write out the first letter of each word in the passage somewhere you can reference it throughout the week as you work on your memorization.

Use a whiteboard to write out the passage. Erase a few words at a time as you continue to repeat it aloud. Keep erasing parts of the passage until you have it all committed to memory.

CREATE

If you can, make up a tune for the passage to sing as you go about your day, or try singing it to the tune of a favorite song.

Sketch the passage, visualizing what each phrase would look like in the form of a picture. Or, try using calligraphy or altering the style of your handwriting as you write it out.

Use hand signals or signs to come up with associations for each word or phrase and repeat the movements as you practice.

SAY IT

Repeat the passage out loud to yourself as you are going through the rhythm of your day—getting ready, pouring your coffee, waiting in traffic, or making dinner.

Listen to the passage read aloud to you.

Record a voice memo on your phone and listen to it throughout the day or play it on an audio Bible.

SHARE IT

Memorize the passage with a friend, family member, or mentor. Spontaneously challenge each other to recite the passage, or pick a time to review your passage and practice saying it from memory together.

Send the passage as an encouraging text to a friend, testing yourself as you type to see how much you have memorized so far.

KEEP AT IT!

Set reminders on your phone to prompt you to practice your passage.

Purchase a She Reads Truth 12 Card Set or keep a stack of note cards with Scripture you are memorizing by your bed. Practice reciting what you've memorized previously before you go to sleep, ending with the passages you are currently learning. If you wake up in the middle of the night, review them again instead of grabbing your phone. Read them out loud before you get out of bed in the morning.

CSB BOOK ABBREVIATIONS

OLD TESTAMENT

GN Genesis	**JB** Job	**HAB** Habakkuk	**PHP** Philippians
EX Exodus	**PS** Psalms	**ZPH** Zephaniah	**COL** Colossians
LV Leviticus	**PR** Proverbs	**HG** Haggai	**1TH** 1 Thessalonians
NM Numbers	**EC** Ecclesiastes	**ZCH** Zechariah	**2TH** 2 Thessalonians
DT Deuteronomy	**SG** Song of Solomon	**MAL** Malachi	**1TM** 1 Timothy
JOS Joshua	**IS** Isaiah		**2TM** 2 Timothy
JDG Judges	**JR** Jeremiah	**NEW TESTAMENT**	**TI** Titus
RU Ruth	**LM** Lamentations	**MT** Matthew	**PHM** Philemon
1SM 1 Samuel	**EZK** Ezekiel	**MK** Mark	**HEB** Hebrews
2SM 2 Samuel	**DN** Daniel	**LK** Luke	**JMS** James
1KG 1 Kings	**HS** Hosea	**JN** John	**1PT** 1 Peter
2KG 2 Kings	**JL** Joel	**AC** Acts	**2PT** 2 Peter
1CH 1 Chronicles	**AM** Amos	**RM** Romans	**1JN** 1 John
2CH 2 Chronicles	**OB** Obadiah	**1CO** 1 Corinthians	**2JN** 2 John
EZR Ezra	**JNH** Jonah	**2CO** 2 Corinthians	**3JN** 3 John
NEH Nehemiah	**MC** Micah	**GL** Galatians	**JD** Jude
EST Esther	**NAH** Nahum	**EPH** Ephesians	**RV** Revelation

BIBLIOGRAPHY

CSB Study Bible. The First Missionary Journey of Paul. Nashville: Holman Bible Publishers, 2017.

CSB Study Bible. The Second Missionary Journey of Paul. Nashville: Holman Bible Publishers, 2017.

CSB Study Bible. The Third Missionary Journey of Paul. Nashville: Holman Bible Publishers, 2017.

Graham, Isabella. *The Power of Faith, Exemplified in the Life and Writings of the Late Mrs. Isabella Graham.* New York: American Tract Society, 1843.

Logos Bible Software. *Paul's Early Travels.* 2009.

McKnight, Scot. *Reading Romans Backwards: A Gospel of Peace in the Midst of Empire.* Waco: Baylor University Press, 2021.

Thielman, Frank. *Romans.* Grand Rapids: Zondervan, 2018.

Webber, Robert. *The Biblical Foundations of Christian Worship,* 1st ed., Vol. 1. The Complete Library of Christian Worship. Nashville: Star Song Publishing Group, 1993.

Never Miss a Day in God's Word

The **She Reads Truth Subscription Box** is an easy way to have a Bible reading plan delivered every month.

We'll send you a Study Book filled with daily Scripture readings and all sorts of beautiful extra features to help you read and understand the Bible. All you have to do is open your book, read with us today, and read with us again tomorrow—it's that simple!

beauty goodness truth

You just spent 35 days in the Word of God!

MY FAVORITE DAY OF
THIS READING PLAN:

HOW DID I FIND DELIGHT IN GOD'S WORD?

ONE THING I LEARNED
ABOUT GOD:

WHAT WAS GOD DOING IN
MY LIFE DURING THIS STUDY?

WHAT DID I LEARN THAT I WANT TO SHARE
WITH SOMEONE ELSE?

A SPECIFIC SCRIPTURE THAT
ENCOURAGED ME:

A SPECIFIC SCRIPTURE THAT
CHALLENGED AND CONVICTED ME: